Foxy Epoxy

Foxy Epoxy

44 GREAT EPOXY CLAY PROJECTS WITH SERIOUS BLING

Kristal Wick

LARK JEWELRY & BEADING

LARK JEWELRY
& BEADING

An Imprint of Sterling Publishing
387 Park Avenue South
New York, NY 10016

ISBN 978-1-4547-0758-5

Distributed in Canada by Sterling Publishing
c/o Canadian Manda Group, 165 Dufferin Street
Toronto, Ontario, Canada M6K 3H6
Distributed in the United Kingdom by GMC Distribution Services
Castle Place, 166 High Street, Lewes, East Sussex, England BN7 1XU
Distributed in Australia by Capricorn Link (Australia) Pty. Ltd.
P.O. Box 704, Windsor, NSW 2756, Australia

For information about custom editions, special sales, and premium and
corporate purchases, please contact Sterling Special Sales at 800-805-5489
or specialsales@sterlingpublishing.com.

Email academic@larkbooks.com for information about desk and examination copies.
The complete policy can be found at larkbooks.com.

Every effort has been made to ensure that all the information in this book is accurate. However, due to differing conditions, tools,
and individual skills, the publisher cannot be responsible for any injuries, losses, and other damages that may result from the use of
the information in this book.

Manufactured in China

2 4 6 8 10 9 7 5 3 1

larkbooks.com

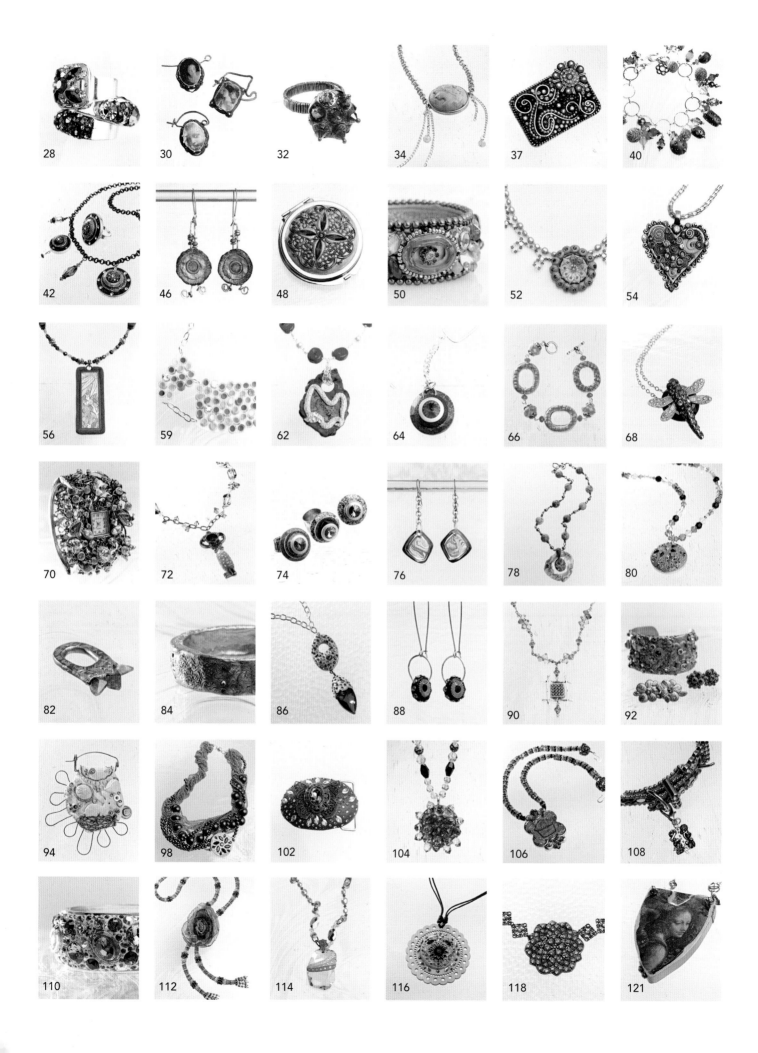

28

30

32

34

37

40

42

46

48

50

52

54

56

59

62

64

66

68

70

72

74

76

78

80

82

84

86

88

90

92

94

98

102

104

106

108

110

112

114

116

118

121

contents

124

128

introduction

...xy *Epoxy*! Prepare to cram, jam, smush, and goosh your way to FAB
...es it easy to make jewelry for all ages, in all color palettes and in every
...op bling! I'll be your tour guide on this journey, along with 12 spectacular
... instructions to make bracelets, pendants, earrings, belt buckles, key

... learn the fundamentals of epoxy clay, a material that's non-toxic, simple
...ft chains and online. It requires no expensive equipment, firing, or baking.

...gratification material for jewelry making. You can mix a batch of your own
... it with a splash of chatons or a dab of resin here, a dash of pearls and a
...g out the door bedecked in your new pieces in 24 hours. But a word of
...u know how to mix up a batch of this magical stuff, no blank surface will

...r from the range of terrific projects our fabulous and foxy jewelry
...heck out Andrew Thornton's Crystal Cave Ring (page 82), Margot Potter's
...ng (page 59), and Christina Orlikowski's Dragonfly Brooch (page 68). If
...elegant pieces incorporating image transfers (pages 30 and 121) or her
...btler side of epoxy clay.

...h inspirational pieces sure to get your creative juices flowing and have you
...k of epoxy clay. So, hop on board, crank up some inspiring tunes, and join
...velry-making life!

Creatively yours,

Kristal

basics

Epoxy clay is my new best friend, and it's about to become yours! With this product you don't need expensive equipment to make fabulous jewelry—no kilns, no torches. Leap right into the wonderful world of epoxy clay and wear your first creation tomorrow!

EPOXY CLAY

Epoxy clay is self-hardening and comes in two parts. Part A is epoxide (a resin) and part B is polyamine (a hardener). To use the clay you simply knead equal amounts of parts A and B together—no firing or heating is necessary. The clay comes in a wide range of colors and there is zero shrinkage. Once cured, epoxy clay is permanent, even under water. It's very hard and durable but will break like glass or ceramic if dropped on a hard surface.

Epoxy clay was invented and used for the automotive/aviation/home repair world and was once found only in hardware stores. It doesn't bleed or seep, so it can fill holes and cracks that come into contact with water and not soften. Epoxy clay adheres to all the clean surfaces I've tried: wood, metal, ceramic, fiberglass, foam, glass, plastics, and stone. You can still find the basic stuff in hardware stores, but the craft and sculpture worlds have hopped aboard the bandwagon and it's now available at craft stores, bead shops, and online.

TECHNIQUES

Let's jump right in and look at the techniques you'll use to make the pieces in this book. (You'll find more on the materials and tools starting on page 16.)

WORKING WITH EPOXY CLAY

Always use a liberal application of hand lotion, cream, balm, or olive oil, or wear disposable gloves before you mix epoxy clay to prevent the clay from sticking to your hands. If you wear gloves, be sure to throw them away when moving on to a different color. Dip your tools in cold water to keep the clay from sticking to surfaces.

You should follow the manufacturer's instructions for each brand of clay to mix the two parts, but it's usually simply a matter of kneading equal amounts of A and B together. The best way to make sure you have equal amounts of A and B is to roll each into a ball and then compare the balls side by side. The time needed to mix is typically two to four minutes.

Once you mix a batch of clay, let it sit for a few minutes. Then mold it into the desired shape or insert it into a blank component. You have roughly two to three hours to work with the clay before it starts hardening. It will fully cure to a semigloss finish in 24 hours. See Working Time Line (above right) for more details on the various stages of the clay as it sets and cures.

Clues from Kristal

Be sure to clean your fingers or tools so you don't cross-contaminate parts A or B in their containers.

WORKING TIME LINE

0–30 minutes:	Very sticky
1–2 hours:	Most beneficial time to shape and mold the clay
2–3 hours:	Clay starts setting up, good time to carve details or stamp
4–24 hours:	Curing time
24 hours:	Completely cured and waterproof

You can cover large areas with clay very quickly or work in smaller, more detailed areas, mixing up small batches of the clay to add to partially or fully cured clay. Sand, tap, drill, carve, and lathe away once the clay is fully cured without chipping or cracking it (be sure to wear a dust mask and safety glasses when sanding or grinding). Epoxy clay can be painted wet or dry.

Epoxy clay cures faster in a warm environment than in a cold one, and you can speed the process by using a heat gun. You can also preheat a craft oven, regular oven, or toaster oven to 150°F (65.6°C), turn it off, and put your epoxy clay creation inside for 15 minutes.

Cleanup is easy with soap and water but remember that epoxy clay is used to fix plumbing leaks. Keep alcohol-based disposable wipes handy and use them on your hands and tools and to wipe off excess clay before washing so the clay doesn't go down the drain where it could clog the pipes once it cures (some brands clean up easier with cold water). Leftover epoxy clay can be frozen to extend the shelf life of one year.

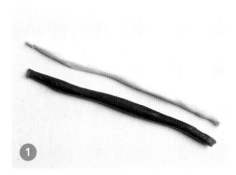

MIXING CUSTOM COLORS

Here are the basic steps to mix custom colors for epoxy clay:

1 Flatten two or more colors of epoxy clay A into pancakes, one on top of the other.

2 Knead the pancakes together thoroughly with your fingers until you have one solid color, and then shape it into a ball.

3 Shape a ball of epoxy clay B that's the same size as the mixed ball of epoxy clay A.

4 Knead the ball of epoxy clay B with the ball of epoxy clay A until the entire ball is a solid color.

OMBRE

To create what I call an ombre effect (see photo, above), roll out a small to medium ball of colored epoxy clay A (I used orange in the example shown) and divide it into three balls. Add a small ball of white epoxy clay A to one of the colored balls and mix. Add a larger ball of white to a second ball of colored epoxy clay A and mix; repeat with a larger ball of white for the third orange ball. When you're satisfied with the shades of colored balls, add an equal amount part B to each ball of A, and mix them according to the manufacturer's instructions. Roll out a long snake of the darkest shade and gently smush it onto your surface. Repeat with the other two shades with the lightest at the top and gently smooth out the edges with your fingers until you're pleased with the effect.

MARBLING

Knead a batch of colored clay parts A and B, following the manufacturer's instructions. Knead a batch of white clay, parts A and B, following the manufacturer's instructions. Shape each color into a snake . Twist the snakes together ❷. Fold the snake in half, twist again, and flatten and shape ❸ —or shape directly into your blank, bezel, or crystal ring.

USING RESIN

Jeweler's grade resin is a two-part epoxy resin that, when you mix equal parts together, cures to a permanent clear glass-like state that does not fade or yellow. It's completely waterproof and takes three days to fully cure, but you can wear it in 24 hours (for those immediate gratification–oriented folks like me). You can create a matte finish by using fine sandpaper and a buffing cloth once it's set up. The resin can also be drilled and carved. A big plus with the jeweler's grade resin is that you rarely have any air bubbles if you mix it in a warm room, follow the manufacturer's directions, and let the resin sit for five minutes after mixing before you pour.

UV curing resins are premixed so you simply pour straight from the bottle and set it in the sun or cure it under a nail lamp for 15 to 20 minutes. You can eliminate air bubbles by poking them with a toothpick before curing or by quickly waving a butane torch flame over the bubbles, which should make them rise to the surface and disappear.

Clues from Kristal

Feel free to do your nails and UV resin curing at the same time— that's multitasking at its finest!

Resin

Two-part mold putty

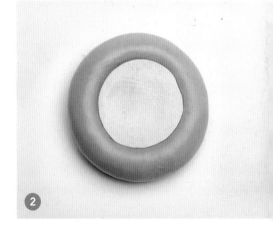

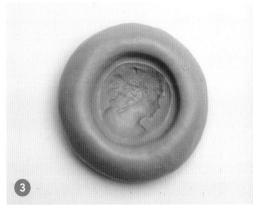

MAKING MOLDS AND CASTING

With two-part silicone mold putty, it's easy to make your own molds and then cast cabochons and cameos with epoxy clay. The process is quite simple, but because the putty sets up quickly, make sure you have the object you're going to use to make the mold (the cameo in this example) clean and ready before you start. Each brand comes with slightly different instructions, but here are the basic steps:

1 Shape equal parts of silicone putty A and silicone putty B into two balls, making sure that, once combined, you'll have enough mold putty to surround your object with at least an extra ½ inch (1.3 cm) of putty around the sides and the bottom.

2 Knead together until parts A and B are thoroughly mixed and one solid color, but don't overknead or your putty will start to harden and won't be moldable. Shape the putty into a ball and then flatten it on a craft mat ❶.

3 Carefully push your object into the putty ❷. Let it cure according to the manufacturer's directions (usually 10 to 20 minutes).

4 Remove the object from the mold, and the mold is ready to use ❸.

5 Now knead a ball of mixed epoxy clay that will fill the mold cavity, push it evenly into the mold.

6 Smooth and flatten the side of the clay that faces up and let the clay cure completely (three to four hours) before removing it.

Opening and closing jump rings

figure 1

BASIC JEWELRY TECHNIQUES

OPENING AND CLOSING JUMP RINGS

Grip the jump ring on both sides of the split using chain- or flat-nose pliers. Rotate one hand toward you and the other away from you so you are twisting the ring open, not pulling the ends apart. Close the jump ring using the same motion, making sure the split is closed tightly.

SIMPLE LOOPS AND BEAD LOOP LINKS

Practice makes perfect when it comes to making loops, so if you're new to jewelry making, just keep on looping and you'll have professional-looking loops in no time!

1 String bead(s) onto a length of wire (or a head pin). Use chain-nose pliers to bend the wire at the top of the bead to a 90° angle ❶.

2 Cut the head pin, leaving about ½ inch (1.3 cm) of wire—the length depends on how large a loop you desire ❷.

3 Grasp the end of the wire with round-nose pliers and rotate the pliers to form a loop ❸. Tweak the loop if needed to center it.

4 To make a bead loop link (figure 1), simply repeat these steps to enclose a bead (or beads) between two loops.

WRAPPED LOOPS AND WRAPPED BEAD LOOP LINKS

1 String bead(s) onto a length of wire (or a head pin) and leave 2 inches (5.1 cm) or more of wire above the last bead. Use chain-nose pliers to make a 90° bend in the wire ¼ inch (6 mm) from the top of the bead ❶.

2 Grip the wire at the bend with round-nose pliers and shape the wire over the top jaw to form a partial loop ❹. Reposition the pliers so the bend is in the bottom jaw, then swing the wire underneath to form a loop ❺.

3 Now wrap the wire around the stem by pulling the wire around with your fingers or chain-nose pliers until you reach the bead ❻. Trim any excess wire and use the chain-nose pliers to gently squeeze the wire end to tuck it in.

4 To make a wrapped bead loop link (figure 2), simply repeat these steps to enclose a bead (or beads) between two wrapped loops.

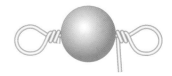

figure 2

CRIMPING

Crimp tubes are great for attaching findings to beading wire. The jaw of a pair of crimping pliers has two notches: one is U shaped and the other is oval.

1 String a crimp tube and then the finding onto the wire. Thread the wire back through the crimp tube in the opposite direction.

2 To secure the crimp tube, fit the crimp into the U-shaped notch (the notch furthest from the pliers' tip) and squeeze **7**.

3 Rotate the crimp tube 90° and place it inside the oval notch. Squeeze the pliers so the crimp tube folds in on itself into a nicely shaped tube **8**.

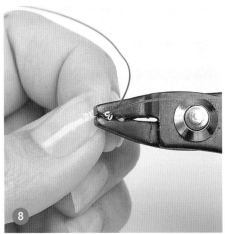

MATERIALS

I'll bet you already have a lot of the supplies called for in these projects (and if you're like me, you welcome an excuse to try new ones). Here's a closer look at some of the materials the designers and I really love to use.

PAINTS, INKS, PIGMENT POWDERS, AND PASTES

Epoxy clay comes in many different colors and you can mix to create your own custom colors, but you may also want to use acrylic paints, inks, pigment powders, and rub-on paste to enhance your epoxy clay creations.

ACRYLIC PAINTS

Acrylic paints come in a wide variety of colors and finishes; my all-time favorites are the metallics with their added glimmery sheen. They feature an easy soap-and-water cleanup, and you can use the paint right out of the bottle full strength or water it down a tad for a wash effect.

ALCOHOL INKS

Alcohol inks are acid-free permanent inks that dry quickly and produce a shiny, metallic effect that works great on epoxy clay. The inks are translucent, so layering different colors and using them with acrylic paints creates stunning effects. You can dilute the inks with rubbing alcohol or use them straight from the bottle.

To make your own alcohol inks, dump some powdered dye (adjust the amount to the color intensity desired) into a small jar with a tight-fitting lid, pour rubbing alcohol to the top of the jar, close the lid, and shake really well until the powder is dissolved as much as possible. Keep shaking from time to time so the powder stays suspended in the liquid and doesn't settle to the bottom.

PEARLIZED ACCENT INKS

Pearlized accent inks go on smoothly and dry the same vibrant color you started with. Their lovely pearlized sheen can be used with the other products discussed here for intense accents.

PIGMENT POWDERS

Pigments powders come in many colors—I love the metallics, of course! Brush them on dry to add a translucent shimmer to clay surfaces. You can also layer different colors for fun effects.

RUB-ON PASTES

There are several types of rub-on paste available for coloring and finishing epoxy clay, and those that add a metallic finish can be buffed to a shine. A popular brand is Gilders Paste, which is a combination of wax, resin, and pigments for coloring metal, wood, ceramics, and more. It can be rubbed onto the surface with the fingers, a sponge, a brush, or a cloth. It can also be thinned with paint thinner for brush application. It comes in a variety of colors, both matte and metallic.

SMOOTHING SOLVENT

Smoothing solvent can be used to smooth out any cracks or fingerprints on the clay. It's also great for cleaning up sticky residue the clay may leave on your fingers or tools.

ADHESIVES

For most of the projects in this book, crystals, beads, and other embellishments are embedded in the epoxy clay, which forms a permanent bond when cured. However, a few things do need to be glued.

TWO-PART EPOXIES

Use two-part epoxies following the manufacturer's directions to permanently bond a variety of surfaces.

MULTIPURPOSE ADHESIVES

Multipurpose adhesives are available at craft stores and hardware stores. They dry quickly to a clear, hard bond.

WATER-BASED GLUES

These adhesives have no chemical solvents, so they are safe to use in areas that aren't well ventilated (like your craft room in the middle of winter).

SILICONE MOLD PUTTY

It's easy to make your own cabochons (such as the cameo on page 34) from epoxy clay if you use two-part silicone mold putty to create a mold. The two-part material is easy to mix and makes casting simple. See page 13 for more on making molds.

RESIN

Resin dries to a clear, hard mass and can be used to embed beads, charms, and found objects. There are two types of resin I enjoy using: UV cure resin and air-dry self-leveling jeweler's grade resin. UV cure resin is used straight from the bottle. Jeweler's grade resin is a two-part epoxy that you mix before using.

BEADS AND SUCH

Bead, beads, beads—I could go on forever about these beloved little beauties. They come in dozens of shapes, sizes, and colors and are perfect for embellishing epoxy clay.

SEED BEADS

Seed beads range in size from less than a millimeter to several millimeters. The lower the number, the larger the bead. The largest size of a seed bead is 1° ("one-aught," sometimes written 1/0) and is 3 mm, and the smallest is 24°, about the size of a grain of sand. The most commonly used seed beads for epoxy clay are sizes 8°, 11°, 12°, 13°, and 15°.

CRYSTAL BEADS

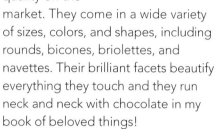

My favorite crystal beads are manufactured by Swarovski in Austria and are the highest quality on the market. They come in a wide variety of sizes, colors, and shapes, including rounds, bicones, briolettes, and navettes. Their brilliant facets beautify everything they touch and they run neck and neck with chocolate in my book of beloved things!

CHATONS

My favorite crystal chatons are manufactured by Swarovski in Austria as well. These cone-shaped crystals have a beveled top edge and a metal foil backing, which causes a stunning reflection. Chatons are easy to push into epoxy clay, giving you another reason to fall in love with them instantly.

RIVOLIS

Rivolis are basically large chatons and are also manufactured by Swarovski. They come in a wide variety of shapes, sizes, and colors, with foiled backing to enhance their facets.

PEARLS

Pearls add a touch of elegance wherever they land. There are so many types of pearls to fall in love with, from stick and baroque pearls to dyed pearls; take your pick. I especially adore glass pearls. These imitations of natural pearls have a uniform size and weight—handy when planning out a design—and are uniformly coated with iridescent, mother-of-pearl-type layers, giving them a luminosity and luster just like real pearls.

RING-SHAPED BEADS

Ring-shaped beads, meaning beads that have a large open center, come in a wide variety of shapes, such as hearts, ovals, squares, circles, and triangles. They can be composed of many materials, including metal, crystal, ceramic, gemstone, and more.

CUP CHAIN

Cup chain (also called rhinestone chain, crystal cup chain, or crystal trim) consists of a series of crystals set individually in a brass metal cup-shaped chain setting and comes in a variety of sizes, shapes, and color combinations. The metal cup chain plating comes in gunmetal, gold, sterling silver, and raw (no plating).

FILIGREE COMPONENTS

Filigree components played a large part in art deco and art nouveau designs in the early 1900s. Today's replicas are usually made of 85 percent copper and 15 percent zinc, 100 percent nickel, or lead-free metal and come in a huge array of finishes, including oxidized copper-plated brass, antique silver, copper, matte gold, and matte bronze, to name a few. Filigree components are available in many different shapes. See how incredible they look filled with epoxy clay in Debbi Simon's Vintage Filigree Necklace on page 124.

NAIL HEADS

Nail heads come in many shapes and themes and will add another decorative element to your designs.

SPACER BEADS

Spacer beads are kind of like a comma in a sentence. They add a visual breath to your design.

BEAD CAPS

Bead caps fit on the top and bottom of a bead and look especially lovely on larger beads. They come in many shapes, depths, and finishes. You may have to "audition" a few to see how they fit into your finished piece.

BLING!

Use glitter, mica, and microbeads to add bling to any project.

GLITTER

Glitter is some fun, folks! It's the gift that keeps on giving—the stuff seems to go everywhere no matter how careful you are, and you'll be surprised how long it keeps popping up long after you've closed the lid! But you can't argue with its delightful results. There are quite a few glitter types out there these days, such as fine, opaque, transparent, dust, and my favorite: German Glass Glitter. It's big and chunky, reflects the most light, and leaves an interesting texture. All types of glitter can be used with resin.

MICA

Mica, a rock formation mineral that flakes off in thin transparent sheets, comes in a variety of colors and sizes from ultra-fine dust to regular powder. I like to use the powder and rub it onto still-uncured epoxy clay. You'll get a beautiful shimmery glow that you can layer with any number of rubbings for a custom color finish.

MICROBEADS

Microbeads are tiny glass marbles around 0.5 mm in size. Don't spill these bad boys or your vacuum cleaner will forever hold a grudge! Always pour glitter, mica, or microbeads over a sheet of paper so you can fold the paper in half and carefully pour the excess back into the container.

Clues from Kristal

I strongly suggest testing some of these products to make sure you're happy with the results before using your precious bezel or blank for the final masterpiece.

by gauge numbers: the lower the number, the thicker the wire.

STRINGING MATERIALS

The material you use to string your jewelry has a big impact on the overall design and feel of a piece. Metal wire, beading thread, and beading wire are some of the more popular choices.

METAL WIRE

Silver wire and gold wire are commonly used for jewelry making, but I suggest trying some of the colorful craft wires to add an extra element to your epoxy clay designs. This wire has a copper base with a non-tarnish enamel coating that's very durable so you can wrap and coil away! Wire diameter is measured

BEADING THREAD

There are a number of great beading threads out there with as many ongoing debates as to which is the "best" one. Because I work so much with crystals, I mainly use a braided beading thread such as WildFire or FireLine. Crystals' sharp edges can cut other threads easily, so you may want to stitch through your crystals twice for added strength.

BEADING WIRE

Beading wire is used for stringing and is made of multiple strands of stainless steel covered with nylon. It's firm enough to be used without a needle and comes in a wide variety of colors, finishes, and thicknesses.

BEZELS AND BLANKS

Bezels and blanks are key to your epoxy clay projects. A bezel is any type of empty chamber that you can smush clay into. You'll find ring, bracelet, earring, and pendant bezels in many different finishes from bright

and shiny to antique. Blanks are usually a flat surface onto which you can add your epoxy clay creations. As with bezels, you'll find them for everything from rings to pendants. Some bracelet blanks are plain metal cuffs or even empty masking tape rolls. Some blanks are open-backed (without a solid backing). Whatever style you choose, you'll have endless fun filling these blanks and bezels with epoxy clay creations.

FINDINGS

Each project will list the findings needed for that piece, but here are some of the main ones you'll want to have on hand when making epoxy clay jewelry.

CLASPS

These include toggles with a toggle bar, lobster clasps, hook and eye sets, box clasps, and torpedo clasps. Magnetic clasps are fun to embellish with epoxy clay and chatons.

EARRING FINDINGS

Ear wires, lever backs, and posts are the most commonly used earring components with epoxy clay designs.

CRIMP COVERS

These provide a great, simple, and attractive way to hide your crimps.

END CONES

End cones come in handy when you want to hide a messy gathering of beading wire ends.

BAILS

Pinch, hinge, loop, and prong bails all allow you to easily dangle a top-drilled bead or pendant from a necklace.

JUMP RINGS

These little wire rings are easy to open and close and can be used to link components, dangles, chain, and other findings.

CHAIN

Chain has become the latest "metal buffet" in the beading and jewelry-making world. For most of the projects in this book, you can substitute your choice of chain.

TOOLS AND EQUIPMENT

You don't need a lot of fancy tools to work with epoxy clay and make the projects in this book, but here are some that will come in handy.

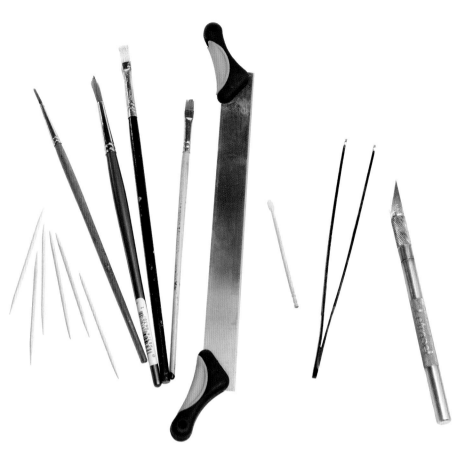

DISPOSABLE GLOVES, DISPOSABLE WIPES, AND HAND CREAM

These are essential for protecting your hands when working with epoxy clay. Gloves or hand cream (or even oil) will keep the clay from sticking to your hands, and wipes can be used to clean clay from hands, tools, and bezels and blanks.

SILICONE NONSTICK CRAFT SHEETS

These mats are the perfect surface for working with epoxy clay. The clay will stick to most other surfaces permanently.

Clues from Kristal

Freezer bags also make a great portable work surfaces. They leave a smooth surface on the back of your clay creations, and you can smush and goosh all you want and still get easy nonstick removal once the clay is dry.

POKING, PAINTING, SLICING, JAMMING CRAMMING, AND CUTTING TOOLS

TOOTHPICKS

Strong, thick toothpicks are handy for scooping both parts of epoxy clay out of their containers. Small pointy toothpicks are great for stippling and making marks in the clay to show where to push in a chaton.

PAINTBRUSHES

Use small paintbrushes for detail painting. Use inexpensive disposable brushes for applying sealer.

TISSUE BLADES AND CRAFT KNIVES

Tissue blades and craft knives are thin, sharp aluminum slicing blades that make nice clean cuts in epoxy clay.

CLAY CUTTERS

Clay cutters (cookie cutters) are made of metal and come in many different shapes and sizes. You can find them in the clay and cake decorating aisles of craft stores. I've also found exceptional selections in kitchen and baking stores.

TWEEZERS OR BEESWAX APPLICATORS

Tweezers are mighty helpful when picking up chatons and jamming and cramming them into the clay. A beeswax applicator—a small ball of sticky beeswax on the end of a little stick—is also a favorite for the same task (see photo, page 11). You can make your own by sticking a small ball of picture-hanging putty on the end of a coffee stirrer, toothpick, or shish kebab skewer.

PLIERS AND CUTTERS

Bending, twisting, and snipping—you'll need a range of hand tools to get these jobs done right.

CHAIN-NOSE PLIERS

Chain-nose pliers are a must in your jewelry-making toolbox. They're used for many tasks, such as opening jump rings and wire wrapping loops ❶.

ROUND-NOSE PLIERS

Round-nose pliers are used for making loops in head pins and eye pins and for wire wrapping ❷.

FLAT-NOSE PLIERS

Flat-nose pliers help bend wire and hold it steady as you wire wrap or make simple loops ❸.

WIRE CUTTERS

Flush wire cutters are used to trim craft wire, beading wire, head pins, and eye pins ❹. Side cutters are intended to cut 20-gauge and finer wire. They cut the wire at a slight angle as compared to flush wire cutters, which cut the wire perfectly straight and leave no burrs or sharp edges.

CRIMPING PLIERS

Crimping pliers are used with crimp beads to fix wire strands together ❺. (See page 15 for crimping instructions.)

MISCELLANEOUS HANDY TOOLS

Here are a few tools you may not have already that you'll find handy when making some of the projects in this book.

METAL STAMPS

Use metal stamps to hammer an impression into a flat metal piece. They come in many fun designs and also letters, so you can spell out anything your little heart desires!

METAL FILES

Metal files come in a wide range of grits and sizes. You may find a small file helpful for getting into tight crevasses and for smoothing rough edges.

BENCH BLOCK AND CHASING HAMMER

Use a bench block and chasing hammer to shape, flatten, and harden wire forms. Steel bench blocks are common, but you could also consider using a rubber block that will absorb the noise and vibration when hammering.

HEAT GUN

You can use a heat gun (also referred to as an embossing or craft heat gun) to speed the epoxy clay curing process. Heat guns look like small hair dryers, but they get much hotter, so be sure to use your heat gun on a heat-resistant surface or mat—away from children and pets.

Bench block

Chasing hammer

the project designers

June Beach is the owner and designer of Beach Haus Designs, The June Beach Collection, and the Beach Princess Jewelry collections. She's been designing jewelry and teaching jewelry design and merchandising classes for more than 20 years. One of the original 27 Swarovski ambassadors, June has appeared on the television show *Beads, Baubles and Jewels*. Her work has appeared in *Seventeen* magazine, *People Style Watch*, *Woman's World*, *Canadian Beading*, *Art Jewelry*, *Jewelry Affaire*, *Somerset Studio*, *Bead Design Studio*, and *Belle Armoire Jewelry*. Visit beachhausdesigns.com.

Jean Campbell writes about, teaches, and designs beadwork. She is the senior editor of *Beadwork* magazine and is a Swarovski ambassador. Her books include *Creating Glamorous Jewelry with Swarovski Elements*, *The Art of Beaded Beads*, *Steampunk-Style Jewelry*, and *Beading with Crystals*. Visit jeancampbellink.blogspot.com.

Candie Cooper is a jewelry designer who is inspired by her extensive travel and years living in China. Candie is the author of *Necklaceology*, *Metalworking 101 for Beaders*, *Felted Jewelry*, and *Designer Needle Felting*. She hosts the Public Television series *Hands On* and has appeared on *Beads, Baubles and Jewels*. She earned a B.A. in Art Education and Fine Arts from Purdue University. Visit candiecooper.com.

Stephanie Dixon (aka The Dixon Chick) is a designer and teacher specializing in wire techniques. Living in Toronto, Ontario, she is currently one of two Canadian Swarovski ambassadors. She says she was the first to introduce Crystal Clay to the Canadian market after being hypnotized by it thanks to creator Debra Saucier. Stephanie is a member of the Toronto Bead Society, the Grand River Bead Society, and the West Toronto Beading Guild. Visit thedixonchick.blogspot.com.

Katie Hacker is the host of the public television program *Beads, Baubles and Jewels*. She writes books, contributes to magazines, teaches beading workshops, and is the creator of Katiedids Channel Findings, which are manufactured by Beadalon. She is a Swarovski ambassador. Katie lives in rural Indiana with her family. Visit katiehacker.com.

Katerina Ilieva was born in Bitola, Macedonia, which has a long tradition of handicraft, music, and folklore. Today she lives and works in Singapore. In 2004 she discovered beading, and later she discovered epoxy clay. Her business is called KI Jewelry. Visit katerinailieva.com.

the project designers

Christina Orlikowski of Evergreen, Colorado, is a full-time artist working in a variety of media, from oil and pastel painting to jewelry featuring pearls, semiprecious gems, and metal clay. Her work is often inspired by the textures and colors of the Colorado landscape. She's a member of the Plein Air Artists of Colorado, the Pastel Society of Colorado, the Art Students League of Denver, and the Evergreen Artists Association, and she is a founding member of Artists With Altitude. She teaches metal clay at the Center for the Arts in Evergreen. Visit chrisorlikowski.com.

Margot Potter is an author, designer, freelance writer, and TV host residing in the Smoky Mountains of East Tennessee. Margot has written seven books on jewelry making and has designed and consulted for many jewelry making and craft industries. She is a Swarovski ambassador. She creates bimonthly vintage-inspired blog posts for iLoveToCreate and is a member of the Beadalon Design Team. Visit margotpotter.com.

Debra Saucier is a mixed-media artist who has been beading since summers spent with her grandmother in Japan as a child. Debra is a Swarovski ambassador. In 2006, Debra and her husband opened a small bead store called The Bead & Wire Shop. In 2011, Debra launched a new product called Crystal Clay, a two-part epoxy clay. Her work was featured in *Beading Across America*. Visit debrasaucier.blogspot.com.

Brenda Schweder of Waukesha, Wisconsin, is the author of *Steel Wire Jewelry*, *Junk to Jewelry*, and *Vintage Redux*. Her work has been featured in many books and magazines, including *30-Minute Earrings*, *30-Minute Necklaces*, *30-Minute Rings*, *30-Minute Bracelets*, *Chains Chains Chains*, *Art Jewelry*, *Wirework*, *Step by Step Wire*, *BeadStyle*, *Bead&Button*, *BUST*, *Vintage Style Jewelry*, and *Steampunk-Style Jewelry*. She is a Swarovski ambassador and has served as president of the Loose Bead Society of Greater Milwaukee. Visit brendaschweder.com.

Debbi Simon is an artist, teacher, and author who has been working creatively since 1993. Her original jewelry designs have been published in numerous magazines and books, and she is the author of *Crystal Chic*. Her paintings have been exhibited in juried and invitational shows. A Swarovski ambassador, she teaches workshops and demos in resin, epoxy clay, and crystals. Visit dsimonfineart.com.

Andrew Thornton is a professional fine artist who left New York City for rural Pennsylvania. His work can be seen in private collections around the globe. Andrew works part time with his family at Green Girl Studios. A regular contributor to books and magazines, he is also the creative director of the bead store and art gallery Allegory Gallery in Ligonier, Pennsylvania. See more of his work at andrew-thornton.blogspot.com and allegorygallery.com.

by Kristal Wick

bling rings

These rings are so quick and easy to make you'll have one in every color in no time. Great gifts for your gal-pal-blingistas!

MATERIALS (for one ring)

- Epoxy clay
- 1 silver ring blank with built-in channel
- 20 to 50 chatons in a variety of shapes and colors, sized from 1 to 6 mm

TOOLS

- Hand cream or disposable gloves
- Nonstick surface
- Tweezers or beeswax applicator (optional, for picking up chatons)

1 Roll out a small ball of epoxy clay A and add an equal amount of epoxy clay B. Mix according to the manufacturer's instructions.

2 Roll the clay into a ball, then smush it into the center chamber of the ring blank.

3 Using the tweezers or a beeswax applicator to pick up the chatons, jam and cram the chatons into the clay in a random design.

4 Let the clay fully cure.

5 Repeat to make as many bling rings as your heart desires!

vintage bezel
pins

Just unearthed from years buried in a secret garden or granny's attic, these pieces, inspired by old Roman pins, look like the real deal.

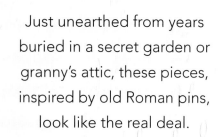

by Debbi Simon

MATERIALS

- Small color photocopy (see Tip)
- Vintage-style bezels, 1 to 1½ inches (2.5 to 3.8 cm)
- White epoxy clay
- Approximately 4-inch (10 cm) length of 18-gauge brass or copper wire per bezel (see Note)
- A variety of crystals and beads
- Brass or copper head pins

Note: If you substitute a different gauge wire, make sure it's not too thick, as this wire will go through clothing when the pin is worn.

TOOLS

- Hand cream or disposable gloves
- Nonstick surface
- Scissors
- Metal spoon
- Bowl of room-temperature water
- Heavy-duty flush wire cutters
- Round-nose pliers
- Bench block and hammer
- Lighter (optional, see Make the Pin, step 3)
- Flat-nose pliers

Fill the Bezel and Transfer the Image

1 Trim the color photocopy to match the size of your bezel with a little overlap.

2 Roll out a small ball of white epoxy clay A and add an equal amount of epoxy clay B. Mix the clay according to the manufacturer's instructions. Roll the mixed clay into a ball, push it down into the bezel, and stretch the clay out into the surface of the bezel, being sure to push the clay into the corners. Work until the bezel cavity is almost full and the surface is nice and even. Stretching the clay as opposed to compressing it to fill the bezel will leave the clay tackier, and it will take the transfer better.

Tip Debbi used copyright-free images of Renaissance art. The transferred image will be the reverse of the original image, so if orientation is important, scan and flip the image on your computer before making the working copy. Laser or toner-based printer copies usually work best for image transfer. If you only have access to an inkjet printer, test an image from it on a scrap piece of epoxy clay first.

3 Place the color photocopy in the desired position face down onto the freshly mixed clay in the bezel.

4 With the back of a metal spoon, burnish the color photocopy to the clay. Set the piece aside and let it cure for at least three to four hours, if not overnight.

5 After the clay has cured, use your fingers to dab water liberally onto the back of the photocopy on top of the clay and then allow it to sit for five minutes.

6 Dab more water on the paper and start rubbing your fingers over the back of the copy, removing the wet paper. The color image is left behind on the clay as the paper is being removed. Continue adding water and rubbing until all the paper is removed.

Make the Pin

1 Decide on the pin shape and sketch it out to scale. Debbi looked through old images of Roman pins for inspiration.

2 With wire cutters and round-nose pliers, cut and shape a length of wire to the desired shape.

3 Place the wire form on a bench block and use a hammer to add texture to the wire, flattening some areas and leaving others round. Be sure to keep a point for the part that will be going through clothing. If desired, use a lighter to oxidize the wire, making it look a little more aged.

4 Add extra detail and sparkle to the bezel with crystals and beads strung onto head pins and attached to the bezel with a simple or wrapped loop (see page 14).

5 Repeat the steps to make a variety of pins. Follow the instructions for the Cameo Necklace (see page 34) to mold vintage metal stampings, and then add the molded pieces to a few bezels.

wire wrapped
rings

For a touch of stylish whimsy, make a few of these in every color and you'll have a new wardrobe! These would also make fun napkin rings for your party guests to wear home.

by Andrew Thornton

MATERIALS (for one ring)

- 10½ inch (26.7 cm) length of 18-gauge dead soft copper wire
- 1 bead cap, 18 to 21 mm, or size of your choice
- 1 copper ball head pin
- 44-inch (1.1 m) length of 24-gauge dead soft copper wire (use square wire for a crisper look)
- Liver of sulfur
- Microcrystalline wax polish
- Black epoxy clay
- Assortment of crystal chatons, rhinestones, bicones, and vintage sequins
- Gold pigment powder

TOOLS

- Hand cream or disposable gloves
- Nonstick surface
- 2 pairs of chain-nose pliers
- Ring mandrel
- Wire cutters
- Microcrystalline foam polishing pad
- Soft cloth
- Tweezers or beeswax applicator (optional, for picking up chatons)
- Dust mask
- Soft brush

Note: The materials listed are enough to create one ring.

tip For a variation on the crystal chatons, string a crystal bicone and a vintage sequin onto a copper ball pin and make a wrapped loop (see page 14). Insert the wire-wrapped loop of the dangle into the clay. Repeat with six more components to give the ring a sea urchin effect.

1 Use the chain-nose pliers to form a curl on one end of the 18-gauge wire. Thread the other end of the wire through the inside of the bead cap so the curled wire is contained in the bead cap.

2 String the bead cap onto a head pin so the cap cups the head pin. Then hold it (facing up) tightly against the ring mandrel, and wrap the wire around the mandrel one size up from the desired ring size. Wrap the wire twice more around the mandrel, flanking either side of the original wrap for a total of three coils. Wrap the wire "tail" around the base of the bead cap; trim if desired.

3 Remove the ring armature from the mandrel. Hold 3 inches (7.6 cm) of the length of 24-gauge wire and wrap the remainder twice around the base of the bead cap tightly. Using the pliers, hold the three coils of the ring base flush and wrap the longer end of the 24-gauge wire around the ring "band" to secure the thinner wire onto the thicker, and start the coiling of the band. Wrap the shorter 3-inch (7.6 cm) tail around the base of the bead cap, trim if necessary, and tuck the tip of the wire into the coils.

4 Continue to tightly wrap the 24-gauge wire around the armature band, being sure to use pliers to hold the wires flush while wrapping. Move the pliers as you go. If you don't use the pliers, the shape of the ring will distort! Use the second pair of pliers to help wrap the wire firmly.

5 When the band has been completely covered, wrap the end of the 24-gauge wire around the base of the bead cap, trim, and tuck the end into the wraps so it doesn't poke you.

6 Patina the copper wire with liver of sulfur, following the manufacturer's instructions. Dry it completely and polish with a polishing pad. Use a soft cloth to apply microcrystalline wax polish to the ring and buff it.

7 Roll out a small ball of black epoxy clay A and add an equal amount of epoxy clay B. Mix the epoxy clay according to the manufacturer's directions. Roll it into a ball and insert it into the bead cap. Press down lightly. Using the tweezers or the beeswax applicator, apply stones such as chatons in a pattern.

8 While the clay is still tacky, don the dust mask, and lightly dust the clay with gold pigment powder using a soft brush. When the clay has cured fully, buff it with a soft cloth to remove excess powder.

This is epoxy at its finest.
Mold your own cameo out of epoxy
clay and then pretend it came
from an archeological dig.

by Debbi Simon

cameo
necklace

MATERIALS

- 1 vintage cameo, 1¼ inches (3.2 cm) in diameter (see Note)
- Two-part silicone molding material (see page 16)
- Colorants (oil or acrylic paint, pigment powders, and rub-on paste)
- Epoxy clay in blue, green, and white
- 1 bezel with two attaching loops to fit your cameo
- 24- to 36-inch (61 to 91.4 cm) length of silver chain, 8 mm
- 4 silver jump rings, 5 mm
- 12-inch (30.5 cm) length of a smaller, finer silver chain, 2 mm
- 2 to 4 silver head pins
- 2 to 4 crystals or other beads

Note: Please make sure the cameo you use to make the mold is copyright free.

TOOLS

- Hand cream or disposable gloves
- Nonstick surface
- Small paintbrush (optional)
- Sanding tool (file, sandpaper, or emery board)
- Round-nose pliers
- Chain-nose pliers
- Wire cutters

Make the Mold

1 Clean and thoroughly dry the cameo so it's ready to use for making the mold. (See page 13, Making Molds and Casting.)

2 Measure out small balls of equal size of both parts of the silicone molding material and mix them together according to the manufacturer's instructions. Quickly roll the mixed putty into a ball and press it down onto a flat surface until it's the thickness of your cameo.

3 With the flat side up, push the cameo a little more than halfway down into the putty; be careful not to push too far down into the material so you have plenty of floor for the mold and the cameo doesn't press through the bottom. Bring the mold putty up around the sides of the cameo until it's even with the back all the way around. Let the mold sit undisturbed until it's fully cured, usually five to 15 minutes, and then remove the cameo from the mold.

Make the Cameo

1 Using your finger or a brush, lightly add color to the raised areas inside the mold. Debbi likes to use oil or acrylic paint, pigment powders, and rub-on paste. For an aged patina look, try a burnt sienna or a brown sepia tone.

2 Make a ball of teal-colored epoxy clay A that's half the amount needed to fill the mold by mixing blue epoxy clay A with a little green and a little white epoxy clay A until you achieve the desired color.

cameo necklace

3 Shape a ball of epoxy clay B equal to the amount of teal epoxy clay A, and mix the two parts together according to the manufacturer's instructions. Form a ball that will fill the mold cavity, and then push it evenly into the mold, trying not to move the clay around so much that you disturb the color in the raised areas of the mold.

4 Smooth and flatten the side of the clay that faces up and let the clay cure completely (three to four hours) before removing it.

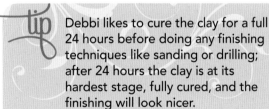 **tip** Debbi likes to cure the clay for a full 24 hours before doing any finishing techniques like sanding or drilling; after 24 hours the clay is at its hardest stage, fully cured, and the finishing will look nicer.

5 Finish the clay cameo by sanding down the edges and flattening the bottom until it fits into the bezel. You can do this with a file, sandpaper, emery board, or any metalworking sanding tools you have.

 tip If you don't want to use a bezel, you could drill a hole in the pendant and add it to a chain with a jump ring.

6 Once the cameo fits into the bezel, mix another small batch of epoxy clay (the color doesn't matter), and put a very thin coat in the bottom of the bezel. Push the clay cameo into the bezel, adhering it to the layer of wet clay. Once the cameo is secure in the bezel, set it aside to cure fully.

7 When the seal has cured, attach the bezel to your chain. Attach one end of the thicker chain to one of the bezel loops with a jump ring, using two pairs of pliers to open and close the ring, and then attach the other end of the chain to the second bezel loop with another jump ring.

8 Cut the smaller, finer chain into varying 1- to 2-inch (2.5 to 5.1 cm) lengths. Use head pins and a simple loop (see page 14) to add a few accenting crystals or beads to one end of one or two chains. Then use a jump ring to attach two or three lengths of chain to one of the bezel loops. Repeat, attaching the rest of the chain lengths onto the second bezel loop. The piece shown has three lengths on one side and two lengths on the other side for an asymmetrical look. Feel free to customize to your taste.

western bling
belt buckle

Combine vintage and current
components with wire wrapping and
epoxy clay and the result is this spectacular
belt buckle. Scour flea markets for vintage costume
jewelry to add to the bling.

by Christina Orlikowski

MATERIALS

- Black construction paper
- 1 large rectangular silver belt buckle blank, 3 x 1¾ inches (7.6 x 4.4 cm)
- 15-inch (38.1 cm) length of tarnish-free 16-gauge silver wire
- 31-inch (78.7 cm) length of tarnish-free 22-gauge silver wire
- Approximately 45 assorted silver spacer beads, 1.5 mm, 2 mm, and 3 mm
- Black epoxy clay
- Approximately 135 assorted clear, clear AB, black, pink, orange, red, and purple foil-backed chatons from 1 to 4 mm (see Note)
- 12 to 14 flat gunmetal spacer beads, 6 mm
- 1 Western concho with rhinestones, 36 mm

Note: This project looks best if you use round chatons mostly but sprinkle in other assorted shapes.

TOOLS

- Hand cream or disposable gloves
- Nonstick surface
- Scissors
- Flush wire cutters
- Round-nose pliers
- Rawhide mallet
- Rubber block
- Tweezers or beeswax applicator (optional, for picking up chatons)

western bling belt buckle

1 Cut out a rectangle the size of your buckle from the black construction paper. Trim the paper to fit the inside of the buckle—this will allow you to test your design against a black surface.

2 Cut two pieces of 16-gauge wire, each about 5 inches (12.7 cm) long. Using round-nose pliers and one length of wire, make a spiral at each end to create an S shape; repeat so that you have two similar pieces.

3 Cut a third piece of 16-gauge wire about 12 inches (30.5 cm) long. Using round-nose pliers, make a spiral at each end to create a very long S shape. Make two hairpin turns near the center of the S shape so that you end up with a large L shape with spirals at each end. Lay all three pieces into the buckle so that the end spirals meet. Gently shape the wires until they fill the space—be sure to leave space in the upper right corner where you'll attach the rhinestone concho. Because the ends of the wires will be hidden in this corner, you may make these spiral ends smaller or trim anything that will be hidden by the concho.

4 Use the rawhide mallet to gently hammer all three pieces on the rubber block to harden and shape the metal. Lay the pieces into the buckle blank again and adjust as necessary.

5 Cut two 5-inch (12.7 cm) lengths of 22-gauge wire and wrap the spiral shapes together where they meet, wrapping each connecting section about four times. Trim and tuck in the ends. You should now have one large shape that fits easily into your buckle blank, allowing room to add the embellishments.

6 Next you'll add the silver spacer beads to the design. Start by cutting three 7-inch (17.8 cm) lengths of 22-gauge wire. Starting from the bottom left corner, wrap one end of the wire around the large wire framework, string silver spacer beads in a graduated strand long enough to reach the top spiral, and wrap the other end around the framework to attach it. Trim and tuck in the ends.

7 Create two more graduated strands of silver spacer beads to attach along the top and bottom of the framework, gently shaping the wire to follow the curve of the framework. Wrap the ends to attach, and then trim and tuck in the ends. Test the piece once again to make sure it fits inside the buckle.

8 Mix 1 ounce (28 g) of black epoxy clay A with 1 ounce (28 g) of epoxy clay B according to the manufacturer's instructions.

9 Remove the construction paper and start pushing the clay into the belt buckle. Smooth the clay with water (see Tip) and your fingers to make a smooth domed surface about ⅛ to ³⁄₁₆ inch (3.1 to 4.7 mm) deep. Press the completed metal framework into the epoxy clay until the entire piece is partially embedded in the clay.

 tip While I usually use solvent to smooth clay, Christina finds that water works, too.

10 Using leftover clay, make five small balls about the size of a pea and make one large ball about the size of your thumbnail. Set these aside.

11 Making sure you leave spaces for the balls of clay you just made and for the concho, add chatons around the framework by pushing them into the clay, following the shapes of the spirals; use different shapes of chatons to fill the corners and different colors to create patterns.

12 Add the five pea-size balls of clay to your design in the spots you left for them, creating raised surfaces and adding dimension to the piece. Push larger chatons into the balls, slightly flattening the balls. You may attach flat gunmetal spacer beads under some of these balls, allowing the edges to show.

13 Place the large ball of clay in the upper right corner and push the stem of the rhinestone concho into the ball, pressing until the clay spreads and creates a secure attachment. The concho should overlap the edges of the buckle.

14 Make any necessary adjustments to the piece, then set it aside to allow the clay to cure.

My version of transformer jewelry. It's a bracelet. No, it's a necklace. No—a bracelet! Attach this bracelet's S-hooks to a chain or silk ribbon and—bling—you've got a necklace!

by Kristal Wick

charmalicious
bracelet/necklace

MATERIALS

- Blue epoxy clay
- 36 head pins
- 80 to 90 chatons in shades of blue, 1 mm to 4 mm
- Copper and gold mica
- Silver glitter
- A variety of blue, copper, and silver beads, crystals, spacers, bead caps, and charms in various sizes
- 6- to 7-inch (15.2 to 17.8 cm) length of silver chain with large and small links
- 2 S-hook clasps, 1 inch (2.5 cm)
- Silver chain or silk ribbon of desired length (optional, as an extender)

TOOLS

- Hand cream or disposable gloves
- Nonstick surface
- Round-nose pliers
- Flush wire cutters
- Tweezers or beeswax applicator (optional, for picking up chatons)
- Small bowls for mica and glitter
- Paintbrush
- Flat-nose pliers

1 Roll out a medium ball of blue epoxy clay A and add an equal amount of epoxy clay B. Mix according to the manufacturer's instructions.

2 Divide the clay into 11 or 12 balls and roll out into various sizes and shapes, mainly round.

3 Stick a head pin through the center of a clay shape and make a simple loop on the end with round-nose pliers. Trim the ends with wire cutters. Picking up the chatons with tweezers or a beeswax applicator if needed, jam and cram chatons into the clay in a random design. Repeat to make six chaton-studded clay beads.

4 Stick a head pin through the center of the remaining five or six balls and make a simple loop on the end. For a few of the balls, brush the mica onto the ball, making sure you brush the mica into all the nooks and crannies. Brush off any excess mica, set aside, and allow the clay to completely cure. For the last few balls, roll and press the ball into a bowl of glitter. Let the clay thoroughly cure.

5 Make 20 to 24 dangles using beads, crystals, spacers, bead caps, and charms by stringing them onto head pins and making a simple loop at the top.

6 Connect all your clay beads and dangles to the bracelet by opening the loop at the top of each head pin, slipping it over a chain link, and closing the loop.

7 Attach an S-hook clasp to each end of the bracelet. Wear the bracelet by linking the S hooks together. Or link the S hooks to a length of chain or silk ribbon and you've got a necklace!

chaton chiller
necklace and ring

by Kristal Wick

I love the striking effect of black, red, crystal, and silver together. This piece always attracts attention, so think twice about wearing it in public if you're an introvert.

MATERIALS (for the necklace)

- Black epoxy clay
- 1 smooth-edge channel finding circle with an inner channel and one hole in the edge, 35 mm (see Note)
- 2 smooth-edge channel finding circles with inner chambers and two holes in the edge, 25 mm
- 11 crystal chatons, 4 mm
- 3 silver eye pins, 2 inches (5.1 cm)
- 1 black and white ceramic ring, 30 mm
- 1 large textured metal ring, 1 inch (2.5 cm)
- 32 red chatons, 2.5 mm
- 16 red chatons, 4 mm
- 2 small textured metals rings, ¾ inch (1.9 cm)
- 2 silver head pins
- 6 crystal bicones, 3 mm
- 4 gunmetal spacers, 6 mm
- 2 crystal briolettes, 8 mm
- 4 gunmetal head pins, 2 inches (5.1 cm)
- 4 silver spacers, 6 mm
- 4 black spacers
- 2 crystal briolettes with stainless steel grommets, 14 x 9.5 mm
- 2 small black textured beads, 4 mm
- 4 red bicones, 4 mm
- 4 black ornate bead caps, 6 mm
- 2 red crystals, 12 mm
- 2 silver beads, 3 mm
- 9 black oval jump rings, 6 mm
- 20-inch (50.8 cm) length of black chain
- Silver textured toggle clasp

Note: This project uses Katiedids channel findings manufactured by Beadalon.

TOOLS (for the necklace)

- Hand cream or disposable gloves
- Nonstick surface
- Toothpick
- Tweezers or beeswax applicator (optional, for picking up chatons)
- Flush wire cutters
- Round-nose pliers
- 2 pairs of flat-nose pliers

(for the necklace)

Make One Large Focal Bead

1 Roll out a small to medium ball of black epoxy clay A and add an equal amount of epoxy clay B. Mix according to the manufacturer's instructions.

2 Roll about three-fourths of the clay into a snake and smush it into the outer chamber of the large circle. Use the toothpick to poke indentations into the clay at the top where the hole is and directly opposite the first indentation; then make three evenly spaced indentations on each side of the ring between the top and bottom indentations.

3 Using tweezers or a beeswax applicator if desired, place crystal chatons into each indentation and gently jam them into the clay. Cut a silver eye pin to ½ inch (1.3 cm) and push it into the hole at the top of the circle so the wire goes into the clay and the loop is snug against the outer edge of the circle. Stipple the clay by texturing it with a toothpick. Set the piece aside.

4 Place the ceramic ring on top of the large textured metal ring. Roll the remaining clay into a ball and smush it into the hole of the ceramic ring. Place the ceramic and metal rings on the center of the large circle prepared in steps 1 through 3. Goosh the clay down so it reaches the large circle. Jam one crystal chaton in the center of the clay, then cram concentric rings of eight small red chatons, eight large red chatons, and eight small red chatons around the center crystal chaton. Let the piece fully cure.

Make Two Small Focal Beads

1 Roll out a small ball of black epoxy clay A and add an equal amount of epoxy clay B. Mix according to the manufacturer's instructions.

2 Divide the clay in half; roll out a snake and smush it into the outer chamber of one of the small metal circles. Push a silver eye pin through the holes in the circle and make a simple loop on the other end with round-nose pliers. Using a toothpick, poke indentations into the clay at the top and bottom where the holes are, then make one indentation on each side halfway between the top and bottom.

chaton chiller necklace

3 Place large red chatons into each indentation and gently jam them into the clay. Stipple the clay by texturing it with the toothpick.

4 Center a small textured ring on the circle. Roll the rest of the clay into a ball, place it in the center of the small textured ring, and smush it lightly. Jam a crystal chaton into the middle of the clay and cram a ring of eight small red chatons around it. Let the clay fully cure.

5 Repeat steps 1 through 4 for the second small circle.

6 Make two dangles for the small circles as follows: Onto a silver head pin string one crystal bicone, one gunmetal spacer, one 8-mm crystal briolette, one gunmetal spacer, and one crystal bicone. Finish with a wrapped loop and attach it to the circle's eye pin when everything is fully cured.

Make the Dangles and Assemble the Necklace
1 Make two large crystal dangles as follows: Onto a gunmetal head pin string one crystal bicone, one silver spacer, one black spacer, one large crystal briolette, one black spacer, one silver spacer, and one black bead. Finish with a wrapped loop at the top.

2 Make two red crystal dangles as follows: Onto a gunmetal head pin string one red bicone, one bead cap, one red crystal, one bead cap, one red bicone, and one silver bead. Finish with a wrapped loop at the top.

3 Attach all the dangles and focal beads onto the chain by spacing them out in a pleasing manner and using jump rings to attach them to the chain, opening and closing the jump rings with two pairs of flat-nose pliers. Attach the toggle and toggle bar to the ends of the chain with jump rings.

chaton chiller ring

MATERIALS (for the ring)

- Black epoxy clay
- 1 smooth-edge base metal circle with an inner channel and one hole in the edge, 35 mm
- 9 crystal chatons, 4 mm
- 1 large black and white ceramic ring, 30 mm
- 1 textured metal ring, 1 inch (2.5 cm)
- 16 red chatons, 2.5 mm
- 8 red chatons, 4 mm
- 1 ring blank, round or oval

TOOLS (for the ring)

- Hand cream or disposable gloves
- Nonstick surface
- Toothpick
- Tweezers or beeswax applicator (optional, for picking up chatons)

(for the ring)

1 Roll out a small to medium ball of black epoxy clay A and add an equal amount of epoxy clay B. Mix according to the manufacturer's instructions.

2 Roll about three-fourths of the clay into a snake and smush it into the outer chamber of the large circle. Use a toothpick to poke indentations into the clay on two opposite sides (top and bottom), then make three evenly spaced indentations on each side of the ring between the top and bottom indentations.

3 Using tweezers or a beeswax applicator if desired, place crystal chatons into each indentation and gently jam them into the clay. Stipple the clay by texturing it with a toothpick. Set the piece aside.

4 Place the ceramic ring on top of the textured metal ring. Roll the remaining clay into a ball and smush it into the hole of the ceramic ring. Place the ceramic and metal rings on the center of the circle prepared in steps 2 and 3. Push the clay down so it reaches the circle. Jam one crystal chaton in the center of the clay, then cram rings of eight small red chatons, eight large red chatons, and eight small red chatons. Let the piece fully cure.

5 Roll out a small ball of black epoxy clay A and add an equal amount of epoxy clay B. Mix according to the manufacturer's instructions. Roll the clay into a ball and place it in the middle of the ring blank. Goosh the finished piece into the clay in the ring blank and let it fully cure.

in the round
earrings

by Candie Cooper

Some jewelry *must* be touched; these earrings are a perfect example. The brilliant color combo exemplifies patina at its best.

MATERIALS

- 12-inch (30.5 cm) length of half-hard 20-gauge sterling silver wire
- 12 silver spacer beads, 5 mm
- 4 gold Czech spacer beads, 5 mm
- Liver of sulfur
- Pumice powder
- 3-inch (7.6 cm) length of aluminum wire mesh ribbon, 20 mm wide
- Blue epoxy clay
- 2 brass washers, ¾ inch (1.9 cm)
- 2 copper jump rings, ⅜ inch (9.5 mm)
- Brown and navy alcohol inks or acrylic paint
- 2 ear wires (commercial or handmade)

TOOLS

- Hand cream or disposable gloves
- Nonstick surface
- Wire cutters
- Round-nose pliers
- Steel bench block
- Chasing hammer
- Brass brush
- Scissors
- Circle cutter, 1 inch (2.5 cm) diameter

1 Cut two pieces of wire 3¾ inches (9.5 cm) long. Make a bend in the center of each wire.

2 String one silver spacer bead, one gold Czech spacer bead, and two silver spacer beads onto each side of the wires. Use round-nose pliers to make twirls at the ends of the wires to keep the beads from falling off.

3 Lay the wire pieces on the steel bench block, and hammer them, being careful to avoid the beads. You can hammer the wires flat or with the round side of the chasing hammer.

4 To give the wires an antique look, dip them in a solution of liver of sulfur. Use pumice powder and water to remove the oxidation from the high points and follow up with a brass brush to shine.

5 With scissors, cut along one side of the wire mesh ribbon to make a sheet.

6 Mix the epoxy clay according to the manufacturer's instructions. Roll out a thin piece and cut two 1-inch (2.5 cm) circles. Push the wire mesh ribbon into the clay circles and trim around the sides of the mesh.

7 If desired, prepare the washers by laying them on the bench block and hammering with the round end of the chasing hammer to create texture. Push one brass washer into the center of each clay circle, then press a closed copper jump ring into the center of each washer.

8 Cut two rectangles from the clay measuring ³⁄₁₆ x ½ inch (4.5 mm x 1.3 cm). Set these aside—you'll put them on the back of the piece in the next step.

9 Slide one silver spacer, one Czech bead, and one silver spacer bead up to the top (bent end) of each wire, leaving one silver spacer bead next to each twirl. Press the circle piece on top of the wires between the beads, and then press the rectangle clay piece on the back to sandwich the wires between the clay (see the photo on the left). Set the clay and wire pieces aside to fully cure.

10 Give the clay circles an antique look with alcohol inks or watered-down acrylic paint, using light brown in the centers and dark navy around the edges. Tint the brass washer as well.

11 Attach the wire and clay dangles to a pair of ear wires.

compact
mirror

by Debra Saucier

More than a girly-girl compact, the ornate touch of decorative filigree, crystals, and mica powder makes this piece sing with gilded glitz. *Très magnifique!*

MATERIALS

- White epoxy clay
- 1 round compact mirror with a 50-mm bezel
- 1 round filigree bezel, 45 mm
- 4 elongated crystal navettes, 15 x 4 mm
- Vintage bronze mica powder

TOOLS

- Hand cream or disposable gloves
- Nonstick surface
- Beeswax applicator
- Soft-bristled makeup brush

1 Roll out a small ball of epoxy clay A and add an equal amount of epoxy clay B. Mix according to the manufacturer's instructions.

2 Roll the clay into a round ball and place it in the center of the compact mirror. Push the clay to the outer edges of the bezel, and then smooth it using a light feathering motion of your fingertips.

3 Place the round filigree bezel onto the clay and press down gently and evenly.

4 Using a beeswax applicator, place the navettes onto the clay between the filigree openings. Press down gently.

5 Using a soft-bristled makeup brush, apply a heavy coating of mica powder onto the entire top of the compact mirror. When the clay has cured, wash the excess mica powder and beeswax off the piece with warm water.

boho vintage
bangle

by Kristal Wick

This cuff was soooooooo much fun to make! It's a great way to use up your orphan beads, and you can make it as elegant or playful as you want—a party on your wrist for sure!

MATERIALS

- 1 bangle blank or cardboard masking tape roll
- Silver acrylic spray paint (optional, see step 1)
- Pink epoxy clay
- Crystals, chatons, pearls, cup chain, crystal buttons, and crystal rivets in various sizes and shapes
- Antique gold mica
- Approximately 96 antique gold glass pearls, 8 mm
- Approximately 96 black chatons, 1 mm
- 7½-inch (19 cm) length of pink glitter ribbon, 1 inch (2.5 cm) wide
- Water-based glue

TOOLS

- Hand cream or disposable gloves
- Nonstick surface
- Tweezers or beeswax applicator (optional, for picking up chatons)
- Small bowls for mica
- Paintbrush

Note: Work in sections—the clay will dry out too quickly to do the whole bracelet at once. Divide the bracelet into four sections; complete one section, apply mica to the clay, and let it cure before moving on to the next section. When all four sections are cured, complete one edge of the bracelet, let it cure, then finish up with the other edge.

tip In a smaller size, these make great napkin rings!

1 If using a tape roll circle instead of a bangle blank, spray it with silver acrylic spray paint, making sure all the surfaces (including the inside) are sealed well.

2 Roll out a medium ball of pink epoxy clay A and add an equal amount of epoxy clay B. Mix according to the manufacturer's instructions.

3 Roll out about 25 balls in a variety of sizes—you'll use these to attach the components to this section of the bangle. Place your largest component down first by putting one of the clay balls between the component and the bangle and gooshing the component down. Repeat for all the components in this section. Use tweezers or a beeswax applicator to pick up the smaller components.

4 Brush mica onto the clay while it's still wet, carefully brushing it into all the nooks and crannies. Brush off the excess mica and let the piece thoroughly cure.

5 Repeat steps 2 through 4 for the remaining three sections of the bangle.

6 To start completing one edge of the bangle, roll out a medium ball of pink epoxy clay A and add an equal amount of epoxy clay B. Mix according to the manufacturer's instructions.

7 Roll the clay into a thin snake and gently smush the clay snake onto one edge of the bracelet. Jam the 8-mm gold glass pearls into the clay, butting them up next to each other.

8 Cram 1-mm black chatons into the clay below and between the pearls (use the photos for reference). Let the clay thoroughly cure, then repeat for the other edge.

9 Glue the ribbon to the inside of the bangle by applying a thin coat of water-based glue and pressing the ribbon into the wet glue. Let it dry and add one or two more thin coats of glue on top of the ribbon for a strong seal.

czech button bling
necklace

by Kristal Wick

Start out with a stunning Czech glass button and you're sure to end up with a masterpiece. I wanted to incorporate a lot of colors so I could wear this piece with every outfit in my closet. Mission accomplished!

MATERIALS

- Pink epoxy clay
- 1 Czech glass button, 25 mm
- 8 blue chatons
- 7 pink chatons
- Antique gold glitter
- 1 silver-plated brass button converter, domed round with two loops, 25 mm
- Two-part epoxy glue
- 52-inch (132 cm) length of bronze 0.018-inch (.46 mm) 49-strand beading wire
- 38 crystal light pink bicones, 4 mm
- 24 gold baroque glass pearls, 8 mm
- 18 gold baroque glass pearls, 10 mm
- 4 crimp beads
- 108 blue bicones, 4 mm
- 72 crystal AB crystal butterfly-shaped beads, 6 mm
- 12 clear crystals mounted in silver-plated pewter, 6.4 mm
- 2 eye pins, 2 inches (5.1 cm)
- 2 end caps
- 2 chain lengths, 2 inches (5.1 cm)
- 4 jump rings (optional, see steps 8 and 9)
- 1 leaf toggle clasp

TOOLS

- Hand cream or disposable gloves
- Nonstick surface
- Tweezers or beeswax applicator (optional, for picking up chatons)
- Flush wire cutters
- Crimping pliers
- Round-nose pliers
- Flat-nose pliers

1 Roll out a small ball of pink epoxy clay A and add an equal amount of epoxy clay B. Mix according to the manufacturer's instructions.

2 Roll the clay into 15 same-sized balls and smush them close together around the edge of the glass button.

3 Jam one chaton, alternating blue and pink, into each clay ball. While the clay is still wet, sprinkle it with glitter. You may have to press the glitter gently into the clay to make it stick. Let the clay thoroughly cure.

4 Glue the button converter to the back of the glass button using the two-part epoxy glue. Let it dry.

5 With wire cutters, cut the beading wire into a 22-inch (55.9 cm) length and a 30-inch (76.2 cm) length. Onto the short length of wire, string one pink bicone, one small pearl, one pink bicone, and one large pearl 18 times, then string one pink bicone, one small pearl, and one pink bicone. String on a crimp bead and then thread the wire back through the crimp bead; crimp both ends of the wire using crimping pliers (see page 15), leaving a small loop at each end.

6 Onto the longer length of wire, string *one blue bicone and one butterfly bead three times; one blue bicone, one mounted crystal; one blue bicone and one butterfly bead three times; and one blue bicone, then pass back through the mounted crystal crosswise to the first pass; repeat from * five more times. String six blue bicones, one small pearl, the first button converter loop, three small pearls, the second button converter loop, one small pearl, and six blue bicones. String **one mounted crystal; one blue bicone and one butterfly bead three times; and one blue bicone. Then pass back through the mounted crystal crosswise to the first pass and string one blue bicone and one butterfly bead three times, and then one blue bicone. Repeat from ** five more times. Crimp both ends of the wire with crimp beads, leaving a small loop at each end as before.

7 With two pairs of pliers, open up an eye pin and insert one end of each strand, then close the eye pin. String on an end cap, then make a wrapped loop with round-nose pliers (see page 14). Repeat for the other end.

8 Attach the chain lengths to the wrapped loops either by opening the end links or by using jump rings.

9 Attach the toggle and the toggle bar to the other ends of the chain lengths either by opening the end links or by using jump rings.

Don't you just heart all
the snazzy colored wire
available? Spiral it, goosh it
into clay, add a bit of bling,
and you're set.

by Kristal Wick

wire spiral snazz
necklace

MATERIALS

- About 24 short lengths of 20-gauge wire in lime, blue, lilac, pink, orange, yellow, and purple
- 1 large copper heart pendant
- Epoxy clay in lime, blue, lilac, pink, orange, yellow, and purple
- Chatons in a variety of sizes and colors
- 20-inch (50.8 cm) length of copper lantern chain
- 2 copper coil end caps
- 1 clasp of choice

TOOLS

- Hand cream or disposable gloves
- Nonstick surface
- Round-nose pliers
- Flat-nose pliers
- Flush wire cutters
- Tweezers or beeswax applicator (optional, for picking up chatons)

1 To make a spiral, put the end of a wire length between the tips of the round-nose pliers. Gripping tightly, rotate the pliers away from you to form a small circle at the end of the wire. Make this circle the circumference of the chaton you'll be placing in it later (see photo).

2 Reposition the pliers and wrap the wire around the circle, starting the second layer of the spiral. Leave open space between the wire and don't wrap too tightly.

3 Place the spiral in the back of the flat-nose pliers. Continue to rotate and reposition the pliers while you finish the spiral. When you're happy with the spiral, cut any excess away.

4 Repeat steps 1 through 3 to make different colors and sizes of spirals.

5 Lay the spirals in the heart chamber, fitting and rearranging until you're satisfied with the layout.

6 Roll out a small ball of one color of epoxy clay A and add an equal amount of epoxy clay B. Mix according to the manufacturer's instructions. Roll the clay into a small ball to fit under one of the spirals.

7 Lift up the spiral; lay down the clay ball and goosh the spiral into the clay. Jam a chaton into the center circle of the spiral, using tweezers or a beeswax applicator if desired. Repeat with the other colors of clay until all spirals are adhered. Add chatons to the edges of the pendant with other small balls of clay. Let the clay thoroughly cure.

8 Slide the lantern chain through the pendant's bail. Using chain-nose pliers, gently compress one end of the lantern chain so it fits into a coil end cap. Squeeze the bottom coil with pliers until it's secure. Repeat on the other end.

9 Attach the clasp to the end caps.

doodle
pendant

by Kristal Wick

Doodles bring out the kid in each of us, so grab your watercolor pencils and let's go! The frame made of epoxy clay embedded with microbeads is fun to make and to wear.

MATERIALS

- Watercolor paper, 1 x 3 inches (2.5 x 7.6 cm)
- 2 pieces of clear glass, 1 x 3 inches (2.5 x 7.6 cm)
- Antique copper frame with pre-soldered jump ring, 1 x 3 inches (2.5 x 7.6 cm)
- Epoxy clay in yellow and green
- Blue microbeads
- 20-inch (50.8 cm) length of green 0.018-inch (.46 mm) 7-strand beading wire
- 36 cultured freshwater baroque bronze pearls, 6 mm
- 16 lapis faceted rondelles, 5 mm
- 12 copper cube beads, 7 mm
- 42 fluorite faceted rondelles, 7 mm
- 8 antique gold metal spacers, 4 mm
- 8 copper square metal spacers, 10 mm
- 4 lapis lantern beads, 14 mm
- 2 powder blue glass pearls, 6 mm
- 2 antique gold crimp tubes
- Antique gold toggle clasp
- Antique gold pinch bail

TOOLS

- Hand cream or disposable gloves
- Nonstick surface
- Pencil
- Permanent fine-point black marker
- Kneaded eraser
- Watercolor pencils
- Water pen or small paintbrush
- Glass cleaner
- Clay cutter
- Small flat dish or paper plate
- Bead stopper
- Crimping pliers
- Flush wire cutters

1 Use the pencil to draw a design on the watercolor paper. Draw over the design with a permanent fine-point black marker, then erase the pencil marks so only the black lines are left. Color in the design with the watercolor pencils. Start with lighter colors first and work up to the darker colors. Let the colors overlap and blend for interesting shades. Apply several light coats of watercolor pencil, adding more until the desired intensity is reached, rather than one very heavy application.

 Stray watercolor pencil marks can be erased with the kneaded eraser.

2 Fill the water pen chamber with water (or wet your paintbrush) and stroke lightly over your colored design— this softens and layers the coloring. Let the watercolor dry completely.

3 Clean the glass pieces with glass cleaner and let them dry completely.

4 Open the tab on the frame and gently pull the top of the frame open. Slip the watercolor between the two glass panels and slide the sandwich into the frame. Close the top and secure the tab.

5 Roll out a small ball of yellow epoxy clay A and add one-third of that same amount of green epoxy clay A. Mix these thoroughly to create lime green and roll the clay into a ball. Add an equal amount of epoxy clay B to the ball, and mix them according to the manufacturer's instructions.

6 Roll out a long snake and butt it up to one side of your frame. Use the clay cutter to slice off any excess clay, then smush the clay gently so it sticks to the side of the frame. Repeat this step for the remaining three sides, working the top edge up to each side of the frame's jump ring. Smooth out the edges.

doodle pendant

7 Pour the microbeads into a dish and then gently jam and cram the microbeads into the clay. Let the clay thoroughly cure.

8 Place a bead stopper on one end of the beading wire and string the following:

- four bronze pearls
- one lapis rondelle
- three bronze pearls
- one lapis rondelle
- one copper cube bead
- three fluorite rondelles
- one antique gold spacer
- one copper square spacer
- one lapis lantern bead
- one copper square spacer
- one antique gold spacer
- three fluorite rondelles
- one copper cube bead
- one lapis rondelle
- three bronze pearls
- one lapis rondelle
- one copper cube bead
- three fluorite rondelles
- one bronze pearl
- three fluorite rondelles
- one antique gold spacer
- one copper square spacer
- one lapis lantern bead
- one copper square spacer
- one antique gold spacer
- three fluorite rondelles
- one copper cube bead
- one lapis rondelle
- three bronze pearls
- one lapis rondelle
- one copper cube bead
- three fluorite rondelles
- one bronze pearl
- three fluorite rondelles
- one copper cube bead
- one lapis rondelle
- three bronze pearls
- one lapis rondelle
- one powder blue pearl

9 Repeat the series in step 8 in reverse. Pull all the components tightly so there is no slack in the beading wire. Remove the bead stopper. Slide a crimp tube onto each end, slide on the toggle and the bar, pass the wire back through the crimp bead, and crimp the tubes with crimping pliers (see page 15). Cut any excess wire if necessary. Position the bail over the two powder blue pearls and insert the top loop of the pendant into the pinch bail. Pinch it closed.

roundabout
necklace

by Margot Potter

MATERIALS

- 4-foot (1.22 m) length of clear acrylic tubing, ¼ inch (6 mm) in diameter
- Epoxy clay in light pink, pink-orange, olive green, light khaki green, dark yellow beige, sky blue, silver beige, and teal
- 5 foil-backed crystal chatons in light peach, peridot, cloudy blue, cloudy white, and light sapphire crystal, 9 mm
- Templates
- 0.08-inch (2 mm) thick acrylic sheet, 8 x 10 inches (20.3 x 25.4 cm)
- Two-part epoxy glue
- 15-inch (38.1 cm) length of silver chain with large links (longer if you'll lose links when you cut it, see step 7)
- 8 silver-toned jump rings, 10 mm
- 1 silver-toned jump ring, 6 mm
- 1 medium silver-toned swivel lobster clasp

TOOLS

- Hand cream or disposable gloves
- Nonstick surface
- Scissors (sharp and sturdy enough to cut tubing)
- Glue dot runner or other temporary adhesive
- Bench block with clamp
- Jeweler's saw with blade
- Workbench grinder, polishing bit for drill, or sandpaper (to smooth acrylic shape edges)
- Permanent marker
- Electric drill with ¹⁄₁₆-inch (1.5 mm) drill bit
- 2 pairs of chain-nose pliers

roundabout
necklace

So contemporary, this masterpiece could hang on your wall as well as your body!

1 Cut the tubing into approximately 80 pieces ranging in size from slightly smaller than ¼ inch (6 mm) to ½ inch (1.3 cm) in length; the cuts can be angled slightly.

2 Using about ⅓ ounce (10 g) of epoxy clay A and epoxy clay B for each color, follow the manufacturer's instructions and mix eight different colors. Use your fingers to form small rolls and shove the rolled clay into each tube, filling 10 tubes with each color. Use the tip of your finger to gently compress the clay and make a small indentation, but avoid leaving fingerprints.

3 Insert the chatons into five coordinating-color clay tubes. Allow the clay tubes to cure on the nonstick surface overnight.

4 Photocopy the three template shapes provided and then cut them out carefully with sharp scissors. Leaving the plastic coating on the acrylic sheet, adhere the templates to the acrylic sheet using a glue dot runner or other temporary adhesive. Attach the bench block to a table or bench and use the saw to cut out the shapes. If the edges are rough or uneven, use a grinder, polishing bit, or sandpaper to smooth them.

5 Mark hole placements at all corners of the shapes using a permanent marker. Drill the holes. After drilling, remove the plastic sheeting from both sides of the acrylic shapes.

6 Following the manufacturer's instructions, use two-part epoxy glue to adhere the cured clay-filled tubes to the shapes, being careful not to overlap the edges or cover the drill holes. Epoxy glue dries fast, so mix up small amounts and work in sections. Allow the glue to dry overnight.

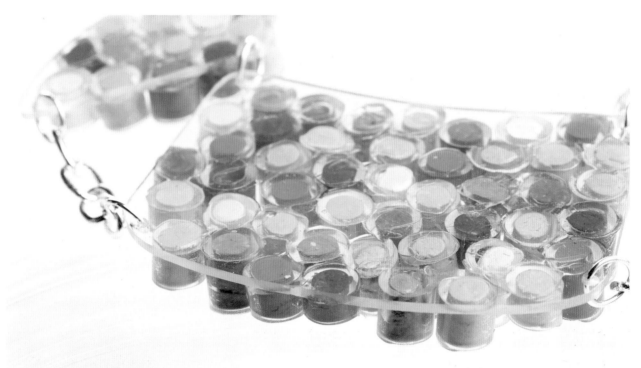

7 Cut the chain into two 6¼-inch (15.9 cm) and two 1¼-inch (3.2 cm) lengths.

8 To assemble the necklace, use two pairs of pliers to open and close the jump rings. Use the 10-mm jump rings to connect the top edges of the segments together, to attach the smaller chain segments to the bottom drill holes between the segments, and to attach the longer chain lengths at the top left and top right drill holes of the smaller shapes. Use the 6-mm jump ring to attach the clasp to one end of a long chain.

templates

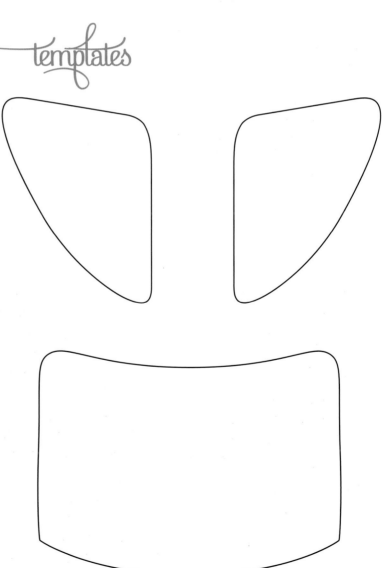

mixed media
necklace

by June Beach

This showstopper is so interesting that it requires close inspection. The subtle reference to chocolate is the secret ingredient!

MATERIALS

- 1 gemstone pendant, 50 to 60 mm
- Printed tape
- Dimensional adhesive glaze or resin
- White epoxy clay
- 98 clear crystal chatons in a variety of sizes
- Pearlescent pigment powder
- 48-inch (121.9 cm) length of 22-gauge non-tarnish silver wire
- 6 coral beads, 8 to 10 mm
- 12 clear bicone crystals, 4 mm
- 4 ivory glass pearls, 6 mm
- 8 clear bicone crystals, 6 mm
- 18-inch (61 cm) length of chain with a rhodium finish

TOOLS

- Hand cream or disposable gloves
- Nonstick surface
- Small paintbrush
- Tweezers or beeswax applicator (optional, for picking up chatons)
- Dust mask
- Brush for pigment powder
- Wire cutters
- Size I (5.5mm) crochet hook
- Chain-nose pliers
- Round-nose pliers

Make the Pendant

1 Clean the surface of the gemstone pendant and let it dry.

2 Tear strips of printed tape and place them onto the pendant. With a small paintbrush, coat the top of the printed tape with dimensional adhesive glaze or resin and allow it to dry thoroughly.

3 Mix a ball of epoxy clay A with an equal amount of epoxy clay B according to the manufacturer's instructions—you'll need an amount large enough to roll out into a snake sized to surround the tape on your pendant. Place the clay around the printed tape to create a frame.

4 Use the beeswax applicator to pick up and place the crystal chatons onto the clay. Repeat until all of the crystals have been placed in the clay, grouping a cluster of larger crystals on one side of the frame.

5 Wearing a dust mask, use the brush to gently dust the pigment powder onto the clay to create a shimmering effect. You can powder as much or as little of the clay as you desire. Allow the clay to cure thoroughly.

Make the Bail

1 Make the bail for the pendant as follows: Cut about 48 inches (121.9 cm) of 22-gauge wire. Using a crochet hook, make a slipknot about 3 inches (7.6 cm) from the end of the wire; with the hook in the slipknot, *wrap the long end of the wire over the hook from back to front; pull the hook with the wire through the slipknot to make one chain stitch. Repeat from * until you have a strand approximately 10 to 12 inches (25.4 to 30.5 cm) long. Cut the wire and use chain-nose pliers to pull the wire end up tight, creating a knot.

2 Wrap the crocheted strand around the pendant and through the opening two or three times to create a bail, bending the wire as needed to get the shape desired.

3 Use round-nose pliers to create a simple wire-wrapped loop (see page 14) at the top of the bail.

Make the Chain

1 Use basic wire-wrapping techniques to create six components of one coral bead and two 4-mm bicones and four components of one glass pearl and two 6-mm crystals using the silver wire; make two lengths with three coral bead components alternating with two glass pearl components, attaching the components with wrapped loops; attach the two lengths together at one end with wrapped loops.

2 Determine the desired finished length of the necklace and attach the required length of chain to the ends of the coral bead components.

by Kristal Wick

guy's
keychain

The guys always seem to get left out when it comes to jewelry, don't they? I put together a keychain with them in mind. Maybe this gift won't get pushed to the back of the sock drawer!

MATERIALS

- 6 large silver jump rings, 12 mm
- 1 ceramic marbled blue ring, 30 mm
- 1 sterling silver keychain
- Blue epoxy clay
- 1 large blue crystal rivet

TOOLS

- Hand cream or disposable gloves
- Nonstick surface
- Chain-nose pliers
- Flat-nose pliers
- Toothpick

1 Using two pairs of pliers, open a jump ring and add it to another jump ring. Repeat with all the jump rings to make a chain.

2 Loop the chain around the ceramic ring and attach the last jump ring to the first jump ring. Open the top jump ring, add the last keychain link, and close the jump ring.

3 Lay the ring flat on the work surface.

4 Measure out a quarter-size portion of blue epoxy clay A and add an equal amount of epoxy clay B. Mix according to the manufacturer's instructions. Roll the clay into a ball and smush it into the center chamber of the ring.

5 Jam the crystal rivet into the middle of the clay, letting the clay ooze out around the rim of the rivet.

6 Stipple the clay with the toothpick. Let the clay fully cure.

by Katie Hacker

aqua daydream bracelet

Got the blues? Here's the perfect bracelet to perk up your day. Comfortable with flip flops or dressed to the nines, this silver and blue combo rocks!

MATERIALS

- 6 silver head pins
- 3 silver oval channel findings, 25 x 30 mm
- Light blue epoxy clay
- Azure blue solvent inkpad
- 6 Caribbean blue opal rondelles, 6 mm
- 6 silver star bead caps, 8 mm
- 3 aqua glass rondelles, 14 mm
- 3 silver eye pins
- 1 silver toggle clasp
- Baby wipe (optional, see Tip)

TOOLS

- Hand cream or disposable gloves
- Nonstick surface
- Cross-hatch rubber stamp
- Round-nose pliers
- Wire cutters
- Chain-nose pliers

1 Pass a head pin through each hole on the oval channel findings with the ends extending outward.

2 Roll out a ½-inch (1.3 cm) ball of epoxy clay A and roll out an equal amount of epoxy clay B. Mix according to the manufacturer's instructions.

3 Roll the mixed epoxy clay into a thin snake.

4 Press the epoxy clay into each oval channel finding, using your fingers to smooth any wrinkles and leaving the clay slightly mounded rather than flat.

5 Ink the rubber stamp and press it onto the clay in each oval channel finding, then set the findings aside to cure.

6 Once the ovals have cured, string a blue opal rondelle onto each head pin.

7 Use the round-nose pliers to bend each head pin into a basic loop; cut off any extra wire.

8 String a bead cap, a 14-mm rondelle, and another bead cap onto an eye pin, then make a basic loop. Repeat to make three beaded eye pins.

9 Use the chain-nose pliers to connect the beaded eye pins and ovals together in an alternating pattern.

10 Connect half of the clasp to each end of the bracelet.

 tip If some of the ink gets on the metal as you're stamping, use a baby wipe to clean it off.

dragonfly
brooch

by Christina Orlikowski

Because of its pin/pendant finding, this dazzling dragonfly can adorn scarves, purses, and jackets. Start with a brass stamping, add a little epoxy clay and cup chain, and you're almost there.

MATERIALS

- Black epoxy clay
- 1 vintage-style antique brass dragonfly stamping, 41 mm tall with 50-mm wingspan
- 1½ inches (3.8 cm) of vintage cup chain with deep pink rhinestones, 3 mm
- 50 assorted foil-backed chatons in a variety of pinks and greens, 1 to 4 mm, including at least 2 large green rounds and 1 large emerald square
- 1 black faceted crystal donut, 30 mm
- Combination pin back/bail finding

TOOLS

- Hand cream or disposable gloves
- Nonstick surface
- Toothpick
- Tweezers or beeswax applicator (optional, for picking up chatons)

1 Mix a ball of epoxy clay A with an equal amount of epoxy clay B according to the manufacturer's instructions—you'll need an amount large enough to roll out into a snake shape about 2 inches (5.1 cm) long and ½ inch (1.3 cm) thick.

2 Mix another ball of clay about the size of your thumbnail and set aside.

3 Roll the large ball into a snake shape and start shaping it around the body and tail of the stamping. The stamping will provide a stiff frame on which to shape the clay.

4 Taper the end of the clay along the tail. Use the toothpicks to shape notches into the clay to simulate the sections of a dragonfly's body and tail. Put a slight curve in the tail. Smooth the clay by wetting your fingers and carefully refining the shape.

5 Attach the cup chain into the clay along the top of the body and along the tail.

6 Place two bright green round chatons for the eyes and place the square emerald green chaton on the top of the head.

7 Press the remaining chatons into the clay along the sides of the body in a symmetrical pattern and place pink chatons along the sides of the tail.

8 Using the small ball of clay, attach the dragonfly to the donut by filling the inside of the donut hole and allowing a small amount of clay to push up and attach to the dragonfly body. Gently push the dragonfly into the clay.

9 Make any necessary adjustments to the piece and set aside. Allow the clay to completely cure.

10 Attach the pin back/bail to the back of the piece using a small amount of clay, adjusting the angle of the dragonfly so that it's on a slight angle. Allow the clay to completely cure.

by Kristal Wick

embellished
watchband

Take any fashion watch and embellish until you run out of room and can still read what time it is. Simply blingalicious, my dears!

MATERIALS

- Purple, green, lavender, and pink epoxy clay
- 1 filigree fashion watch
- 50 to 150 chatons in various shapes, sizes, and colors

TOOLS

- Hand cream or disposable gloves
- Nonstick surface
- Tweezers or beeswax applicator (optional, for picking up chatons)
- Toothpick

1 Roll out a small ball of purple epoxy clay A and add an equal amount of epoxy clay B. Mix according to the manufacturer's instructions. Roll small bits of this clay into balls and smush the balls into some of the crevices of the watchband.

2 Jam chatons into the clay, using tweezers or a beeswax applicator if desired, and stipple the clay around the chatons with a toothpick.

3 Repeat with the green, lavender, and pink clay and more chatons until the watchband is covered.

4 Allow the clay to completely cure.

by June Beach

keys to the sparkle
necklace

Keys unlock mysteries. The key to this statement necklace is crystal chatons, silver glitter, and epoxy clay, along with a cleverly beaded chain.

MATERIALS

- 1 antique silver key pendant, 40 to 45 mm
- Pink epoxy clay
- 70 clear crystal chatons in assorted sizes
- Silver glitter (see Tip)
- 28-inch (71.1 cm) length of cable chain with rhodium finish
- 8-inch (20.3 cm) length of 22-gauge non-tarnish silver wire
- 14 clear AB bicone crystals, 6 mm
- 5 black diamond cubist beads, 16 x 10 mm
- 6 vintage pink bicone crystals, 4 mm
- 4 amethyst bicone crystals, 4 mm
- 3 gray AB bicone crystals, 8 mm
- 17 head pins
- 1 silver toggle clasp
- 2 silver jump rings, 8 mm

TOOLS

- Hand cream or disposable gloves
- Nonstick surface
- Tweezers or beeswax applicator (optional, for picking up chatons)
- Flush wire cutters
- Round-nose pliers
- 2 pairs of chain-nose pliers

 June recommends German glass glitter.

1 Clean the surface of the key pendant and let it dry.

2 Mix the epoxy clay according to the manufacturer's instructions and roll it into a ball. Shape the clay around the long part of the key, covering the area between the head and the lever.

3 Use the tweezers or the beeswax applicator to pick up a chaton and place it into the clay. Repeat until all of the chatons have been placed, then gently press them into the clay.

4 Lightly dust the clay with the silver glitter, and then allow the clay to completely cure.

5 Cut the chain into two 2-inch (5.1 cm), two 4-inch (10.2 cm), and two 8-inch (20.3 cm) lengths. Set the pieces aside.

6 Cut five 1½-inch (3.8 cm) lengths of wire. Use round-nose pliers to make a small wrapped loop (see page 14) at one end of a piece of wire, attaching the loop to a length of chain. String one 6-mm crystal, one cubist bead, and one 6-mm crystal. Trim the other end of the wire with wire cutters and form a wrapped loop, attaching it to another length of chain. Continue making components and attaching them with wrapped loops to chain lengths, creating an asymmetrical chain with five components and two open ends for the necklace's closure.

7 Place each of the remaining 6-mm, 4-mm, and 8-mm crystals onto a head pin and make a simple loop snug to the crystal. Repeat for all the remaining crystals, 17 total. Attach the head pin loops to the chain in random locations.

8 Determine the desired finished length of the necklace and adjust the chain as needed.

9 Attach the toggle clasp to the open chain ends with jump rings, opening and closing the jump rings with two pairs of chain-nose pliers.

rivet
rings

by Kristal Wick

I love ceramic mosaic rings with crystal rivets for an ultramodern look in jewelry design. Use any ring blank or make your own out of metal clay for this stunner.

MATERIALS & TOOLS

- Black epoxy clay
- 1 silver ring blank
- 1 large black and white ceramic fancy stone, 30 mm
- 1 large silver textured metal circle, 1 inch
- 1 black cosmic square ring, 20 mm
- 1 pink crystal rivet, 17 mm
- Hand cream or disposable gloves
- Nonstick surface

1 Roll out a medium ball of black epoxy clay A and add an equal amount of epoxy clay B. Mix according to the manufacturer's instructions.

2 Divide the clay in half; roll each half into a ball and place one ball into the center of the ring blank. Goosh the black and white ceramic fancy stone into the center of the clay.

3 Lay the silver textured metal circle on top of the black and white ceramic stone and smush the other clay ball into the center.

4 Place the black cosmic square ring on top of the clay and jam it down.

5 Place the rivet in the center of the cosmic square ring and jam it into the clay. Set the component upright and then allow the clay to completely cure.

by Kristal Wick

don your jeans earrings

The perfect, most casual pair of earrings you'll ever wear. Colorful jump rings and the blue crystal square rings take these beyond eye-catching!

MATERIALS

- White epoxy clay
- Blue epoxy clay
- 2 blue aluminum jump rings, 12 mm
- 2 blue-green cosmic square ring crystals, 14 mm
- 8 seafoam blue aluminum jump rings, 4 mm
- 6 electric blue aluminum jump rings, 4 mm
- 2 blue aluminum ear wires

TOOLS

- Hand cream or disposable gloves
- Nonstick surface
- Clay cutter
- 2 pairs of flat-nose pliers

1 Roll out a small ball of white epoxy clay A and add an equal amount of epoxy clay B. Mix according to the manufacturer's instructions.

2 Mix a small ball of blue epoxy clay A and add an equal amount of epoxy clay B.

3 Roll out a long snake of each color and place them side by side, then twist them together. Use the clay cutter to cut the snake in half, then roll the two halves together to make another thick snake, then twist them together (see Marbling, page 12).

4 Cut the snake into four even lengths and place them next to each other. Squish the lengths together to create the marbled look.

5 Open a large jump ring with two pairs of pliers and string a square ring crystal. Close the jump ring.

6 Making sure the split in the jump ring is facing the inside of the square so it will be covered by clay, place the square on a flat surface and smush the clay into the open chamber of the square. Be sure to surround the jump ring with clay.

7 Repeat steps 1 through 6 for the other square. Let the clay fully cure.

8 Attach four seafoam blue jump rings and three electric blue jump rings, alternating colors. Attach one end of this "chain" to the large jump ring and the other end to an ear wire. Repeat for the other earring.

geode
necklace

by Kristal Wick

Hard to tell the geode from the epoxy clay on this one! It's fun to pull a theme together and mimic natural elements in epoxy clay. Explore this technique with driftwood, stones, and other gifts of nature.

MATERIALS

- 137-inch (3.5 m) length of antique dark gold 20-gauge wire
- 10 gemstone faceted beads, 20 mm
- 12 gold glass pearls, 6 mm
- 3 gold glass pearls, 4 mm
- 1 antique gold eye pin
- Epoxy clay in white, brown, and black
- 1 large ring-shaped geode, approximately 2 x 2 inches (5.1 x 5.1 cm)
- 1 antique gold lock toggle
- 2 antique gold jump rings
- 1 antique gold pinch bail (sized to fit over the top edge of the geode)

TOOLS

- Hand cream or disposable gloves
- Nonstick surface
- Flush wire cutters
- Round-nose pliers
- Clay cutter
- 2 pairs of flat-nose pliers

1 Cut 10 pieces of wire each 10 inches (25.4 cm) long and use the round-nose pliers to make 10 wire-wrapped links (see page 14) with the 20-mm gemstone beads.

2 Cut 12 pieces of wire each 3 inches (7.6 cm) long. Make 12 simple wire loop links (see page 14) using the large pearls. Make one simple wire loop link using the three small pearls and the eye pin.

3 With the remaining 1-inch (2.5 cm) piece of wire, make a simple wire loop at one end to embed into the clay.

4 Roll out a small ball of white epoxy clay A and add an equal amount of epoxy clay B, and mix according to the manufacturer's instructions.

5 Repeat step 4 to get a small ball of brown clay and a very small ball of black clay.

6 Roll out a long snake of each color, making the black snake thinner than the other colors, place the snakes side by side, and then twist them together (See Marbling, page 12).

7 Cut the snake in half with the clay cutter. Roll the two halves together to make another thick snake, and then twist them together.

8 Cut the snake into four even lengths and place them next to each other. Smush them flat to create a marbled effect.

9 Shape a pendant-size oval of clay to fit inside your ring-shaped geode. Insert the straight end of the wire loop you made in step 3 into the top of the pendant. Allow the clay to completely cure.

10 Attach the links as follows: one pearl link and one gemstone link five times; one pearl link and one three-pearl link; one pearl link and one gemstone link five times; and one pearl link.

11 Add the toggle and the toggle bar to the ends of the necklace using jump rings, opening and closing the jump rings with two pairs of flat-nose pliers.

12 Close the pinch bail over the center small pearl link and the geode ring, capturing the loop of the clay pendant within the bail prongs.

over the moon
necklace

This other-worldly pendant of stippled epoxy clay and crystals shines bright with a shimmery coat of lime green mica powder. If you love blue, try the variation with teal epoxy clay and blue and clear crystals.

by Stephanie Dixon

MATERIALS

- Beige epoxy clay (or teal, see variation)
- Round silver-plated bezel, 37 mm
- 14 khaki crystal bicones, 6 mm
- 4 comet argent crystal bicones, 8 mm
- 6 chrysolite crystal bicones, 8 mm
- 2 chrysolite opaque crystal bicones, 8 mm
- 2 Caribbean blue opal crystal bicones, 8 mm
- 4 clear crystal bicones, 8 mm
- 10 peridot crystal bicones, 4 mm
- 2 jet crystal bicones, 4 mm
- 4 Caribbean blue opal crystal bicones, 4 mm
- 4 palace green opaque bicones, 4 mm
- 2 blue zircon bicones, 4 mm
- 18 olivine crystal rounds, 8 mm
- 12 jet crystal rounds, 8 mm
- 8 large-hole crystal spacers
- Decorative oval magnetic clasp
- Lime green mica powder
- Fine beading wire (6 inches [15.2 cm] longer than the desired length of your finished necklace)
- 2 crimps, 2 mm

TOOLS

- Hand cream or disposable gloves
- Nonstick surface
- Small paint brush
- Crimping pliers

Make the Pendant

1 Roll out a ball of beige epoxy clay A and add an equal amount of epoxy clay B. Mix according to the manufacturer's instructions; the mixed clay should be large enough to fill the bezel to the edges.

2 Using a variety of chatons and fancy stones, create a design in the clay. Ensure that the stone girdles (the edge of the stone table) are covered by the clay. Ladies don't like their girdles showing, and neither do crystals!

3 Once all the stones are set but the clay is still moist, use the paint brush to brush the mica powder all over the pendant. Don't worry if the powder sticks to the crystals: You can use a soft cloth to polish the stones once the pendant has fully cured.

4 Use the toothpick to stipple the clay and allow the color of the clay to show through the mica powder.

Make the Necklace

1 Center the pendant on the beading wire, and string the following:

one khaki bicone, one olivine crystal round, one 8-mm chrysolite bicone, one 8-mm Caribbean blue opal bicone, one jet crystal round, one 8-mm chrysolite opal bicone, one 4-mm comet argent bicone, one 4-mm chrysolite bicone, one palace green opal bicone, one khaki bicone, one clear crystal bicone, one jet crystal round, one olivine crystal round, one spacer, one olivine crystal round, one 8-mm chrysolite bicone, one 8-mm comet argent bicone, one jet crystal round, one 4-mm Caribbean blue opal, three peridot bicones, one khaki bicone, one 8-mm chrysolite bicone, one olivine crystal round, one spacer, one olivine crystal round, one jet crystal round, one khaki bicone, one 4-mm blue zircon bicone, one peridot bicone, one palace green opal bicone, one khaki bicone, one 8-mm comet argent bicone, one jet crystal round, one olivine crystal round, one spacer, one olivine crystal round, one 4-mm Caribbean blue opal bicone, one peridot bicone, one 4-mm jet bicone, one khaki bicone, one clear crystal bicone, one jet crystal round, one olivine crystal round, one spacer, one olivine crystal round, one khaki bicone.

2 String on a crimp bead, add one half of the magnetic clasp, and thread the wire back through the crimp bead. Crimp the end of the wire using the crimping pliers (see page 15).

3 Repeat the stringing order in reverse for the second half of the necklace.

4 String on a crimp bead, add the other half of the magnetic clasp, and thread the wire back through the crimp bead. Crimp the end of the wire using the crimping pliers.

Variation

To make the variation, use teal epoxy clay instead of beige epoxy clay. Instead of green, black, blue, and green crystals, try using varying shades of clear and blue crystals—or feel free to experiment! Give the pendant shimmer with mica powder, or let the clay stand out by itself. If you want to add mica powder, once all the stones are set but the clay is still moist, use the paint brush to brush the mica powder all over the pendant. String the necklace with the same bead colors, or try your own color palette.

crystal cave
ring

by Andrew Thornton

It's amazing what a ball of brown epoxy clay and a little gold pigment powder can do. Such a unique way to use amber crystal pendants, you'll want to stack them to the ceiling!

MATERIALS

- Dark brown epoxy clay
- Olive oil
- 3 organic-cut amber crystal pendants (with holes in the top), 19 mm
- 24 clear crystal chatons, about 2.5 mm
- Gold pigment powder

TOOLS

- Hand cream or disposable gloves
- Nonstick surface
- Chopstick
- Tweezers or beeswax applicator (optional, for picking up chatons)
- Dust mask
- Soft-bristled paintbrush
- Acrylic rolling pin or PVC pipe
- 800-grit sandpaper
- Soft cloth

 Make multiple rings to stack them.

1 Roll out a small ball of dark brown epoxy clay A and add an equal amount of epoxy clay B. Mix according to the manufacturer's instructions. When thoroughly mixed, roll the clay into a ball and place it on the nonstick surface.

2 Press the ball of epoxy clay flat (approximately ¼ inch [6 mm] thick) with the palm of your hand.

3 Coat the chopstick with the olive oil and insert it into the center of the disk of clay. Move the chopstick in an ever-widening oval to accommodate your finger.

 Draw your ring size on the waxed paper with a marker before pressing out the clay and stop expanding the hole when you reach the marker lines. Keep in mind that an oval hole will keep tall rings like this one from turning on your finger. Just turn the ring to the side when slipping it over the joints of your finger and rotate it right side up to put it on.

4 Using your fingers, smooth the edges of the clay. Insert the amber crystal pendants into the top of the ring. Pinch the pendants firmly so that the clay squeezes into the pendant holes and helps lock them into place.

5 Using the tweezers or beeswax applicator, add chatons along the top edge.

6 Create a texture with the end of the chopstick, distressing the surface.

7 Wearing the dust mask and using a soft brush, dust the top with gold pigment powder. Flip the ring over, add chatons, and distress the clay's surface. Use an oiled rolling pin to lightly smooth and flatten the clay. Dust the remaining side and all the nooks with gold pigment powder.

8 Allow the clay to completely cure, and lightly sand it with sandpaper. Always wear a dust mask! Buff the clay with a soft cloth to remove excess pigment and resin dust.

fit-for-a-king
bangle

by Andrew Thornton

Primitively elegant, this bangle is certainly fit for the king, queen, or princess in your life! Inscribe a secret message inside the ornate band for your beloved or an inspirational message to celebrate your inner royalty.

MATERIALS

- 1 bangle blank or cardboard masking tape roll
- Gaffer's tape or strong adhesive tape (optional, see step 1)
- Dark brown epoxy clay
- Gold pigment powder
- 16 brown flat-back crystals, 2.5 mm
- 18 silk-colored flat-back crystals, 4 mm
- Gold acrylic paint
- Rub-on paste (such as Guilders Paste)

TOOLS

- Hand cream or disposable gloves
- Nonstick surface
- 800-grit sandpaper
- Box cutter (optional, see step 1)
- Dust mask
- Soft-bristled paintbrush
- Texturing tool with a carved design or texture sheets

1 Prepare the bangle blank by lightly sanding and cleaning the surface. If you're using a masking tape roll, use the box cutter to remove any excess material to make the roll fit your wrist, then join the ends with the gaffer's tape or strong adhesive tape, smoothing the edges evenly.

2 Roll out a large ball of dark brown epoxy clay and add an equal amount of epoxy clay B. Mix according to the manufacturer's instructions. When the clay is thoroughly mixed, pinch off chickpea-size amounts and apply them firmly to the bangle. Once the outside is completely covered, smooth the surface and even out the shape. Fill any gaps, if necessary.

3 Wearing a dust mask for protection, use the soft brush to powder the texture tool with the gold pigment powder. (The powder will keep the clay from sticking to the tool.) Press the texture tool firmly and evenly into the surface of the clay. If you're using a texture sheet, press and roll it into the bangle. Dust the texture tool or sheet with powder as needed.

 Pressing the texture multiple times over the same spot will make the impression "muddy" and distorted, so if you make a mistake, smooth out the clay first and then press it again.

4 Add the flat-back crystals with the tweezers or beeswax applicator. Place the small crystals so that they flank each larger crystal and are evenly spaced around the bangle.

5 Allow the clay to completely cure. With the sponge, touch up spots with gold paint, and let the paint dry. Antique the bangle by gently dabbing it with rub-on paste, and let it dry. Buff the bangle with a soft cloth.

relic
necklace

by Debra Saucier

Here's a party on your neck! This piece looks complicated but is really quite easy (and fun) to put together.

MATERIALS

- Latte-color epoxy clay
- 1 large oval bezel pendant with loops on the top and bottom
- Approximately 144 assorted yellow, clear, dark blue, and topaz crystal chatons in a variety of shapes and sizes
- 6-inch (15.2 cm) length of gold-colored 22-gauge craft wire
- 1 red crystal pendant, 30 x 14 mm
- 2 gold-colored jump rings, 6 mm
- 20-inch (50.8 cm) length of gold-colored cable chain
- 1 gold-colored lobster-claw clasp

TOOLS

- Hand cream or disposable gloves
- Nonstick surface
- Tweezers or beeswax applicator (optional, for picking up chatons)
- Flush wire cutters
- Round-nose pliers
- 2 pairs of flat-nose pliers

tip Debra likes to rinse her pieces under warm water once they've cured to remove any beeswax.

1 Roll out a medium ball of epoxy clay A and add an equal amount of epoxy clay B. Mix according to the manufacturer's instructions.

2 Roll some of the clay into the bezel pendant, reserving the rest for step 5. Gently pat down the clay so that it's pushed outward to the edges of the bezel. Make sure the bezel is filled and the clay is smooth.

3 Use the beeswax applicator to place the larger chatons into the clay first, spacing them as desired, and then place the smaller chatons to fill the empty spaces. Once all of the chatons have been placed, set the piece aside to fully cure.

4 Insert the piece of wire into the top of the crystal pendant and twist the wire together to secure the pendant. Cut the excess wire, leaving a long enough tail on one side to make a wrapped loop.

5 Place a piece of mixed epoxy clay around the top of the pendant, covering the base of the twisted wire. Embellish the clay with chatons as you did for the oval bezel shape. Once all of the chatons have been placed, set the piece aside to fully cure.

6 With round-nose pliers, create a wrapped loop at the top of the wire that goes through the bottom loop of the oval pendant. Using two pairs of flat-nose pliers, open a jump ring and place the larger section of the two-part pendant onto the ring and then onto the center of the chain. Attach a lobster claw to one end of the chain with the other jump ring.

by Jean Campbell

tire swing
earrings

These elegant earrings made with epoxy clay, crystal rivets, and unique findings resemble a souped-up tire swing—the perfect reminder of easy days gone by.

MATERIALS

- Black epoxy clay
- 2 silver flanged tube findings, 11 x 6 mm
- 20 to 22 clear crystal rivets, 3 mm
- 2 silver hammered jump rings, 20 mm
- 2 silver 1¾-inch (4.4 cm) kidney ear wires
- Solder (optional, see step 4)
- Flux (optional, see step 4)
- Wood sealer (optional, see Tip)

TOOLS

- Hand cream or disposable gloves
- Nonstick surface
- Clay cutter
- 2 pairs of chain-nose pliers
- Soldering iron (optional, see step 4)
- Cheap plastic paintbrush (optional, see Tip)

1 Roll out a small ball of black epoxy clay A and add an equal amount of epoxy clay B. Mix according to the manufacturer's instructions. Roll a snake ¼ inch (6 mm) wide by 2 inches (5.1 cm) long. Use the clay cutter to even the ends.

2 Wrap the clay snake around one tube finding and press it into the channel. Use the clay cutter and your fingers to smooth the ends.

3 Press 10 or 11 crystal rivets into the clay so they are evenly spaced around the circumference of the tube. Smooth the clay as needed; set it aside to cure.

4 Assemble the earring by using one jump ring to connect the tube to an ear wire, opening and closing the ring with two pairs of pliers. If desired, use a soldering iron, solder, and flux to fuse the rings shut.

5 Repeat all the steps to form the second earring.

tip To make the clay shiny, use a cheap plastic paintbrush to paint a coat of wood sealer onto the epoxy clay. Be sure to test the sealer on the crystals, however, before you coat them, too.

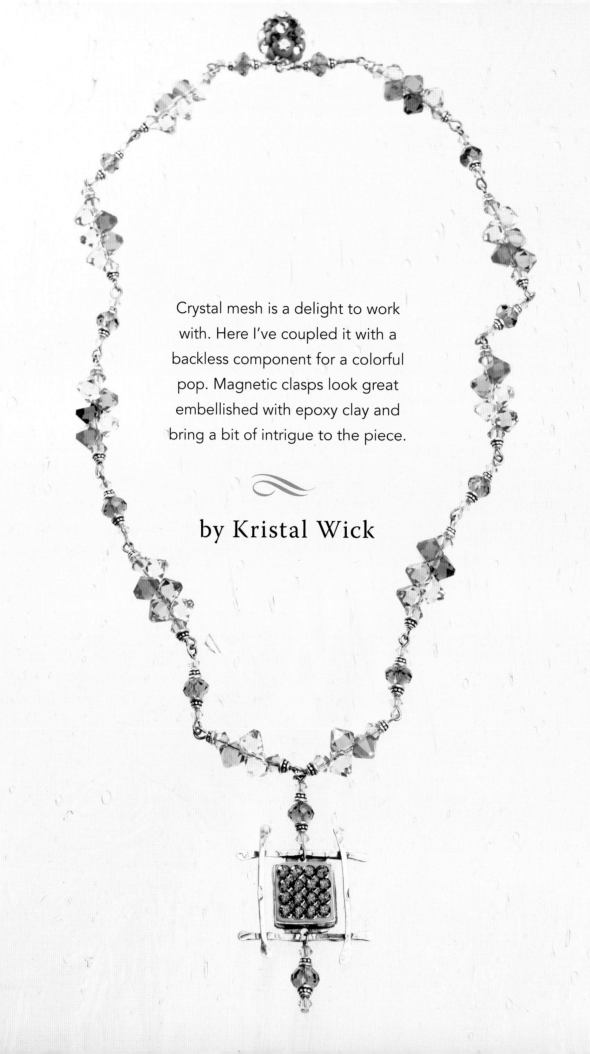

Crystal mesh is a delight to work
with. Here I've coupled it with a
backless component for a colorful
pop. Magnetic clasps look great
embellished with epoxy clay and
bring a bit of intrigue to the piece.

by Kristal Wick

stick pendant
necklace

MATERIALS

- Light green crystal mesh, ¾ inch (1.9 cm) square
- Silver square stick bezel, 2.5 cm
- Lilac and green epoxy clay
- 1 magnetic clasp
- 3 lavender chatons, 4 mm
- 6 lavender chatons, 2.5 mm
- 4 amethyst chatons, 2.5 mm
- 22 silver eye pins
- 24 lavender bicones, 3 mm
- 44 silver bead caps, 4 mm
- 12 green and tan blended briolettes, 6 mm
- 20 light green bicones, 4 mm
- 6 lavender top-drilled bicones, 6 mm
- 10 copper top-drilled bicones, 6 mm
- 9 pale violet top-drilled bicones, 6 mm
- 10 violet top-drilled bicones, 6 mm
- 6 light pink top-drilled bicones, 6 mm
- 5 amethyst top-drilled bicones, 6 mm

TOOLS

- Hand cream or disposable gloves
- Nonstick surface
- Flush wire cutters
- Tweezers or beeswax applicator (optional, for picking up chatons)
- Round-nose pliers
- Flat-nose pliers

1 Use the flush wire cutters to cut the crystal mesh to fit inside the bezel.

2 Roll out a small ball of lilac epoxy clay A and add an equal amount of epoxy clay B. Mix according to the manufacturer's instructions. Smush the clay into the bezel chamber and then press the crystal mesh into the clay. Allow the clay to completely cure.

3 Roll out a small ball of green epoxy clay A and add an equal amount of epoxy clay B. Mix according to the manufacturer's instructions. Roll the clay into very small balls. Place the tiny balls of clay on the magnetic clasp's top; using tweezers or a beeswax applicator if desired, jam and cram the chatons into the clay balls (see the photo below, left). Allow the clay to completely cure.

4 Make 12 components by stringing the following onto an eye pin and using round-nose pliers to form a simple loop at the top: one 3-mm lavender bicone, one bead cap, one briolette, one bead cap, one 3-mm lavender bicone.

5 Make two components by stringing the following onto an eye pin and finishing with a simple loop at the top: one bead cap, one green bicone, three top-drilled bicones, one green bicone, one bead cap.

6 Make eight components by stringing the following onto an eye pin and finishing with a simple loop at the top: one bead cap, one green bicone, five top-drilled bicones, one green bicone, one bead cap.

7 Attach one briolette component to the bottom of the bezel by opening up the loop, inserting the bottom bar of the bezel into the loop, and closing the loop. Attach another briolette component to the top hole of the bezel.

8 Attach the two components with the three top-drilled bicones to the component at the top of the bezel. Onto one of these attach one briolette component and one component with five top-drilled bicones four times, and then one briolette component. Repeat on the other side of the necklace.

9 Open the loops at the end of the necklace with two pairs of pliers and attach the magnetic clasp.

secret garden
cuff and earrings

by Kristal Wick

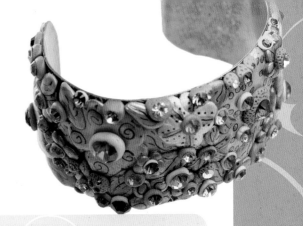

This cuff, inspired by a friend's lush garden, is a chance to let your creative juices flow as you jam, cram, and doodle away. You don't need super painting skills for this project—just add dots, lines, and chatons for a spectacular tiptoe-through-the-tulips experience!

MATERIALS

- 1 metal cuff, 2 inches (5.1 cm) wide
- Epoxy clay in white and various colors
- Acrylic paints in a variety of colors
- Clear acrylic spray
- Chatons in a variety of sizes and colors
- Earring posts and backs

TOOLS

- Hand cream or disposable gloves
- Nonstick surface
- Paintbrushes
- Black fine-point permanent marker
- Tweezers or beeswax applicator (optional, for picking up chatons)
- Toothpick

tip Don't sweat the details! All the details on the piece shown are simple lines, circles, and dots.

Make the Cuff

Note: Work this bracelet in about 1-inch (2.5 cm) sections at a time—the clay will dry out too quickly to do the whole bracelet at once.

1 Size the cuff to your wrist by bending it gently until it fits, putting it on and taking it off your wrist sideways. Make sure the size is right—you won't be able to bend the cuff once the clay has cured.

2 Roll out a small to medium ball of white epoxy clay A and add an equal amount of epoxy clay B. Mix according to the manufacturer's instructions.

3 Make five-petal flowers of different sizes by rolling out five small balls of clay and smushing them in a circular shape together on the cuff.

4 Make leaves by smushing small balls of clay next to the flowers. Repeat until the entire cuff is covered. Allow the clay to completely cure.

5 Paint all the elements with acrylic paints and let them dry, then draw in details with the black permanent marker. Let it dry completely overnight.

6 Spray the cuff with two or three coats of clear acrylic spray to seal the paint. Let the sealant dry completely.

7 Mix a small to medium ball of one color of epoxy clay. Make small balls and smush them on and around the flowers and leaves; using tweezers or a beeswax applicator if desired, jam a chaton into the center of each ball and stipple with a toothpick if desired.

8 Repeat step 7 with the other colors until the cuff is completely covered. Let the clay thoroughly cure.

Make the Earrings

1 Roll out a small to medium ball of white epoxy clay A and add an equal amount of epoxy clay B. Mix according to the manufacturer's instructions.

2 Make five-petal flowers of different sizes by rolling out five small balls of clay and smushing them in a circular shape together.

3 Make leaves by smushing small balls of clay into the flowers. Let the clay thoroughly cure.

4 Paint all the elements with the acrylic paints and let them dry, then draw in the details with the permanent marker. Let it dry overnight.

5 Spray the earrings with two or three coats of the clear acrylic spray to seal them. Let the sealant dry completely.

6 Mix a small ball of one color of epoxy clay. Roll the clay into two little balls and smush them into the center of each flower; jam a chaton into the center of each ball. Let the clay thoroughly cure.

7 Mix a small amount of colored epoxy clay and place a small ball on the back of each flower; goosh an earring post into the clay. Allow the clay to completely cure.

menagerie hare
brooch

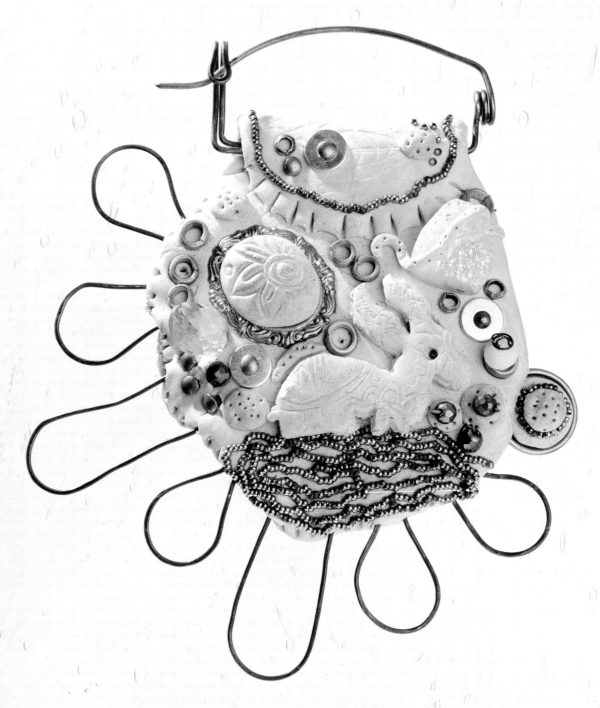

by Brenda Schweder

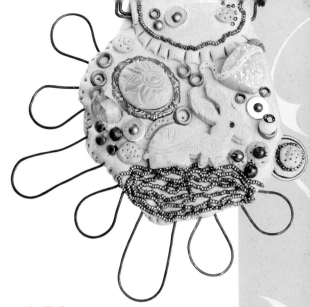

You'll receive plenty of compliments on this brooch with its surprising textures and a bunny peeking out. And it's as fun to make as it is to wear.

MATERIALS

- 30-inch (76.2 cm) length of 20-gauge dark annealed steel wire
- Microcrystalline wax polish
- 18-inch (45.7 cm) length of 28-gauge dark annealed steel wire
- White epoxy clay
- Assortment of found objects
- Assortment of charms, beads, and crystals
- Tiny nails and brads cut down to between ⅛ inch and ³⁄₁₆ inch (3 and 4.5 mm)
- Violet and patina rub-on paste

TOOLS

- Hand cream or disposable gloves
- Nonstick surface
- Jig with ¼-inch (6 mm) and ½-inch (1.3 cm) pegs and mandrels of the same dimensions
- Small utility hammer
- Bench block
- Wire brush or steel wool
- Ruler or measuring tape
- Chain-nose pliers
- Round-nose pliers
- Heavy-duty flush wire cutters
- Needle file
- Small, motorized cutting tool with burr cup (optional)
- Soft cloth
- Awl
- Rabbit cookie or vegetable cutter (a Chinese rabbit vegetable cutter was used for the project shown)
- Small paintbrush

Prepare the Steel Loop Embellishment

1 Set up the jig with six staggered pegs ¼ inch (6 mm) apart on the top and seven staggered pegs ½ inch (1.3 cm) apart on the bottom, and wrap the 20-gauge wire around the top and bottoms of each, forming loops. (Note: If you don't have this many pegs, simply set up as many pegs as possible in the formation, then wind the wire on them all, lift the component, and repeat to make enough loops.)

2 Hammer the piece on the bench block. Clean the component with a wire brush or steel wool and seal it with the microcrystalline wax polish.

3 Pinch the smaller top loops toward each other, fanning the larger bottom loops out.

Prepare the Clay Foundation

1 Roll out a ball of epoxy clay A and add an equal amount of epoxy clay B. Mix according to the manufacturer's instructions. The mixed ball should be about the size of a golf ball.

2 Flatten to more than ¼ inch (6 mm) thick and create an elongated top that's narrower than the opening of your fibula pin.

Add Embellishments

1 Fold the top portion of the clay up and over the bottom wire of the fibula and press it into the lower portion of the clay so that the pin will move freely within the fold. To secure one layer to the other, make little piecrust divots in the clay edge where the two meet with an awl or a similar tool.

2 Press the loopy wire component into the left side and the bottom of the clay component and secure with more piecrust divots.

3 Place the larger found objects and beads, charms, and other original epoxy clay elements (including a rabbit cutout made from a cookie or vegetable cutter) on the brooch form, making small amounts of clay to embed these elements as you go.

menagerie hare brooch

4 Add little round patties and ropes of clay and dot them with an awl.

5 Continue to add small beads, charms, and tiny clay embellishments punctuated by nails and brads and tiny "bobby pins" of steel looped through and around the beads and pushed into to the clay base.

6 Let the brooch cure overnight and then color it with a subtle coat of rub-on paste applied with a small paintbrush.

Make the Steel Fibula (Pin)
1 With the ruler, find the center 2 inches (5.1 cm) of the 28-gauge wire and use the chain-nose pliers to bend a right angle on each side, creating a 2-inch (5.1 cm) lateral section in the center (see figure 1).

tip Smooth the edges to your liking.

2 To form the hook part of the fibula, create a U-bend with round-nose pliers 2 inches (5.1 cm) up on the left side, pinch the parallel lengths together, and then bend a right angle, tracing the first right angle down and across the lateral center section (see figure 2).

3 Wrap the tail around the center section twice and cut the end close to the wrap with wire cutters. Bend the U-bend leg down to create a ⅜-inch (1 cm) hook (see figure 3).

4 Use round-nose pliers to form a spring of three coils parallel to the lateral section and about ⅜ inch (1 cm) above the right angle on the right side (see figure 4).

5 To form the pin part of the fibula, bend a right angle that continues into a curved top about ⅜ inch (1 cm) above the spring. Fit the remaining end under the hook and create an angle that will secure it under the hook (see figure 5).

6 Clip the end just past the hook, then sharpen the tip with a needle file. Use a burr-cup attachment on the small, motorized cutting tool to ball the tip just slightly if desired.

7 Clean the component with a wire brush or steel wool and seal it by rubbing on the microcrystalline wax polish with a soft cloth.

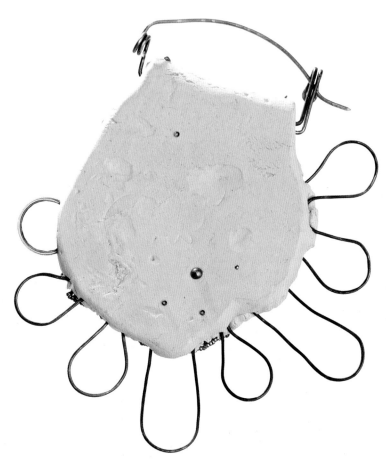

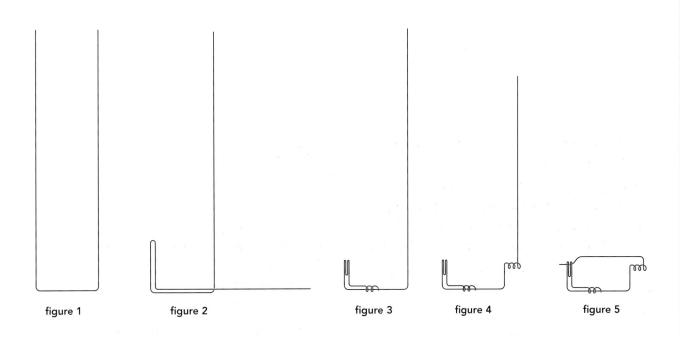

figure 1   figure 2   figure 3   figure 4   figure 5

chunkier the better
necklace

by Debbi Simon

Who doesn't adore the look of chain combined with pearls? A dash of epoxy pavé for sparkle completes the piece.

MATERIALS

- White epoxy clay
- 1 circular bezel pendant with two attaching loops, 38 mm
- 1 sapphire blue crystal chaton, 7 mm
- 6 navette brown crystals, 10 x 5 mm
- 6 pear-shaped dark amber crystals, 10 x 5 mm
- 50 round clear crystal chatons, 2.5 mm
- 72-inch (1.8 m) length of 0.014-inch (0.36 mm) beading wire
- 30-foot (9.1 m) length of stainless steel curb chain, 2 mm
- 6 crimp beads
- 190 dark gray-blue glass pearls, 3 mm
- 100 dark gray-blue glass pearls, 5 mm
- 16 dark brown glass pearls, 10 mm
- 6 jump rings, 5 mm
- 4 jump rings, 8 mm
- Round magnetic clasp, 12 mm
- Two 26-gauge head pins, 1½ inches (3.8 cm)

TOOLS

- Hand cream or disposable gloves
- Nonstick surface
- Straight edge
- Tweezers or beeswax applicator (optional, for picking up chatons)
- Toothpick (optional)
- Alcohol or solvent
- Heavy-duty flush wire cutters
- Crimping pliers
- 2 pairs of chain-nose pliers
- Round-nose pliers

Make the Bezel

1 Roll out a ball of epoxy clay A and add an equal amount of epoxy clay B. Mix according to the manufacturer's instructions. Mix enough clay to fill the bezel and form the clay into a ball.

2 Stretch the ball of clay across the bezel's surface, pushing it all the way to the sides of the bezel. Continue until the clay evenly fills the bezel, making sure you stretch the clay rather than compressing it because stretching the clay will leave it tackier. Don't overwork the clay or it will become less tacky. When the bezel is full, smooth the top of the clay with your fingers to create an even surface.

Add the Crystals

1 With a straight edge, make crosshairs to mark the center of the bezel and help with spacing while you follow the pattern.

2 Using the crosshairs and the photos as a guide, use the tweezers or a beeswax applicator to set one sapphire blue crystal chaton, six navette brown crystals, and six pear-shaped dark amber crystals on the clay. Press the stones into the clay just far enough for the clay to hold them so you can still adjust the stones as needed; you'll push farther in when everything is set.

churkier the better necklace

3 Starting at the bezel edge, start filling in around the stones and along the edge of the bezel with the clear crystal chatons. Continue adding chatons while moving inward to the center of the bezel. Try to space the chatons evenly, using the crosshairs as a guide. Continue until the bezel is filled, completing the process in about 30 to 45 minutes. If working time is closing in and the crystals aren't sticking, make a shallow prick in the clay with a toothpick and then add a crystal.

4 After the bezel is filled completely, gently press down on all the stones until they're embedded in the clay evenly and securely. Make sure the ridges of the crystals are slightly submerged in the clay—things can catch in any space left under the stone and lift the stone out. Clean any residue from the crystals with alcohol or solvent and put the bezel aside to fully cure.

Assemble the Necklace

1 Cut the beading wire into three 24-inch (61 cm) lengths and set aside.

2 Cut the curb chain into nine 36-inch (91.4 cm) lengths and six 5-inch (12.7 cm) lengths and set aside.

3 Use a crimp bead and crimping pliers (see page 15) to attach one end of a 5-inch (12.7 cm) piece of chain to one end of a 24-inch (61 cm) length of beading wire. Repeat to attach one 5-inch (12.7 cm) piece of chain to each of the remaining lengths of beading wire.

4 String 188 glass pearls (3 mm) onto one length of beading wire, reserving two pearls to be used later. Use a crimp bead to attach one end of another 5-inch (12.7 cm) piece of curb chain to the free end of this length of beading wire.

5 Repeat step 4, stringing 100 glass pearls (5 mm) onto another length of beading wire.

6 Repeat step 4, stringing 16 glass pearls (10 mm) onto the remaining length of beading wire.

7 Place each of the beaded wire and chain pieces together with three 36-inch (91.4 cm) lengths of chain. You'll have three four-piece sets that each include three chains and one beaded-wire-and-chain combination.

8 Open a 5-mm jump ring with two pairs of chain-nose pliers and add the end links of one four-piece set. Close the jump ring. Repeat for the remaining two sets.

9 Open an 8-mm jump ring and add the three jump rings from the previous step. Close the jump ring.

10 Begin to braid the three sets of chains together, not too tightly and not too loosely. Once the braid is underway and fairly secure, loosen up the weaving. At random places, leave one length from a set out of rotation and add to the next set. This will create a random design.

11 Continuing braiding until you've used up the lengths, tightening up the braid as you get close to the end.

12 Trim the excess chain and arrange the lengths back into three sets of four chains.

13 Open a 5-mm jump ring and add the end links of one four-piece set. Close the jump ring. Repeat for the remaining two sets.

14 Open an 8-mm jump ring and add the three jump rings from the previous step. Close the jump ring.

15 Open an 8-mm jump ring and add one part of the clasp and one of the 8-mm jump rings holding three sections of chain. Close the jump ring. Repeat this step on the other end.

16 Pass a head pin through a 3-mm glass pearl and one loop on the bezel. Make a loop with the head pin using round-nose pliers to secure it to the bezel. Repeat this step on the other bezel loop.

17 Place the bezel on the appropriate part of the necklace. Open one head-pin loop and attach it to a chain link. Repeat this step with the other head-pin loop, attaching it to a different length of chain so that the bezel lies nicely on the braid.

butterfly belt buckle

by Debra Saucier

Butterflies represent transformation, and what could be more transforming to a strap of leather and blank belt buckle than this fab filigree? Perfect for casual events or a fancy-schmancy soirée.

MATERIALS

- 2 ounces (56 g) of dark brown epoxy clay
- 1 oval filigree bezel, 18 x 13 mm inner diameter
- 1 amethyst oval crystal, 18 x 13 mm
- 1 filigree butterfly, 1½ x 2 inches (3.8 x 5.1 cm)
- 1 oval belt buckle, 2½ x 3 ½ inches (6.4 x 8.9 cm)
- Approximately 75 to 100 chatons in assorted colors and sizes

TOOLS

- Hand cream or disposable gloves
- Nonstick surface
- Wet towel
- Toothpicks
- Tweezers or beeswax applicator (optional, for picking up chatons)

1 Roll out a small ball of dark brown epoxy clay A and add an equal amount of epoxy clay B. Mix according to the manufacturer's instructions.

2 Roll a small amount of the clay into a ball about the size of a pea and place it in the filigree bezel. Place the crystal on top of the bezel and press it into place. Use the wet towel to wipe any excess clay from the sides of the stone.

3 Roll another pea-size ball of clay and place it in the center of the butterfly filigree. Press the oval bezel on top of the butterfly filigree.

4 Roll the remaining clay into an oval. Flatten the oval slightly and shape it over the belt buckle. Smooth the clay using a light feathering motion of your fingertips.

5 Mark the center of the belt buckle with a toothpick. Place the butterfly component onto the center of the belt buckle and smush it into the clay.

6 Place the assorted chatons around the filigree component and jam them into the clay. Allow the piece to completely cure.

by Stephanie Dixon

embedded crystals pendant

Embed crystal pendants in black epoxy clay that's been coated with pewter mica powder, and they'll take on a black, gray, or pewter color, depending on how the light reflects off of them.

MATERIALS

- Black epoxy clay
- Round silver-plated bezel, 37 mm
- Pewter mica powder
- 31 crystal drop pendants, 13 x 6.5 mm
- 10 black polygon crystals, 12 x 8 mm
- 12 crystal faceted round beads, 6 mm
- 16 crystal faceted round beads, 8 mm
- 10 marbled black ceramic round beads, 8 mm
- 6 black bicones, 4 mm
- 30 crystal chatons, 1.8 mm
- Fine beading wire (6 inches [15.2 cm] longer than you want your finished necklace to be)
- 2 crimp beads, 2 mm
- Decorative magnetic clasp

TOOLS

- Hand cream or disposable gloves
- Nonstick surface
- Paintbrush
- Crimping pliers
- 2 pairs of flat-nose pliers
- Wire cutters
- Paintbrush or makeup brush

 tip As you add crystals, the already-inserted ones may start to pop up. As you place the new crystals, continue to press in the previously inserted ones.

1 Roll out a small ball of epoxy clay A and add an equal amount of epoxy clay B. Mix according to the manufacturer's instructions. Press the clay into the bezel to fill it and create a slightly raised dome.

2 Using the paintbrush or makeup brush, dust the pewter mica powder all over the clay, ensuring that there are no missed spots. Blow on the pendant gently to remove any excess mica powder.

3 Embed a crystal drop pendant, hole-end first, into the center of the pendant so that the hole in the crystal pendant is not showing. Continue inserting the crystal pendants around the center one, following the diagrams to the right until you have 21 embedded crystal pendants in all.

4 Further embellish the piece by adding in crystal chatons between the crystals. Ensure that these are well embedded past the mica powder into the clay.

5 Center the pendant on the beading wire and string onto the wire: three small round crystals, one polygon, one large round crystal, one marbled black ceramic bead, one large round crystal, one black bicone, one polygon, one marbled black ceramic bead, one black bicone, five crystal pendants, one black bicone, one polygon, one large round crystal, one marbled black ceramic bead, one large round crystal, one polygon, one large round crystal, one marbled black ceramic bead, one large round crystal, one polygon, one large round crystal, one marbled black ceramic bead, one large round crystal, three small round crystals.

6 String on a crimp bead, and then add a clasp loop and thread the wire back through the crimp bead; crimp the end of the wire using crimping pliers (see page 15). Repeat the stringing order in reverse for the second half of the necklace.

7 String on a crimp bead then add the other clasp loop and thread the wire back through the crimp bead; crimp the end of the wire using crimping pliers.

cowgirl cupcake
necklace

by Kristal Wick

One of my nicknames is Cupcake, so I had to pay homage to my beloved sweet! Make this elaborate herringbone necklace with gumdrop bead caps, or go for the simpler version with chain and a cupcake dangle. Either one is calorie free and brings loads of smiles.

MATERIALS

- Pink decorative paper
- Water-based sealant
- Silver glitter
- 1 decorative pendant blank, approximately 2½ x 1¾ inches (6.3 x 4.4 cm)
- Two-part resin
- 1½-inch (3.8 cm) length of pink cup chain
- Black epoxy clay
- Chatons in a variety of sizes and colors (pink, orange, and clear)
- 2 bead caps
- Beading thread
- Pink and black seed beads, sizes 11° and 8°
- Antique pink crystal bicones, 4 mm
- 2 eye pins
- 1 S-hook clasp

TOOLS

- Hand cream or disposable gloves
- Nonstick surface
- Cupcake punch
- Toothpick
- Tweezers or beeswax applicator (optional, for picking up chatons)
- Clay cutter
- Beading needle
- Round-nose pliers
- 2 pairs of flat-nose pliers
- Flush wire cutters

Make the Pendant

1 Punch out a cupcake from the decorative paper and apply two or three coats of the water-based sealant to each side and the edges. Let it dry.

2 Sprinkle glitter onto the base of the pendant blank.

3 Mix a small amount of two-part resin according to the manufacturer's instructions and pour a small layer on top of the glitter.

4 Place the cupcake on top of the resin and glitter and use a toothpick to push it down into the resin. Allow the resin to completely cure.

5 Mix another small amount of two-part resin and pour it on top of the cupcake, creating a domed effect.

6 Carefully lay the cup chain on top of the resin between the top and bottom of the cupcake and let it thoroughly cure.

Make the Embellishments and Assemble the Necklace

1 Roll out a small ball of black epoxy clay A and add an equal amount of epoxy clay B. Mix according to the manufacturer's instructions.

2 Roll the clay into tiny balls and smush them into the crevices of the pendant, then jam chatons into the clay, using tweezers or a beeswax applicator if desired.

3 Flatten out a ball of clay and use it to cover each bead cap. Trim the clay along the edge of the bead caps and make sure the hole remains open. Jam chatons into the clay, covering most of the bead cap's outer surface. Allow the clay to completely cure.

4 Thread a beading needle with beading thread and make half of the tubular herringbone necklace with a variety of seed beads and the crystal bicones, then stitch a length of 1½ to 2 inches (3.8 to 5.1 cm) using black size 11° seed beads only.

5 Slide the back loop of the pendant onto the black seed bead tube and finish stitching the second half of the herringbone necklace like the first half.

6 Slide an eye pin through the hole of each bead cap.

7 Mix a small amount of epoxy clay and fill each bead cap halfway full; gently stick each end of the herringbone tube into a clay-filled bead cap. Allow the clay to completely cure.

8 With round-nose pliers, make a wrapped loop (see page 14) at the end of each eye pin and attach the S-hook clasp.

diva dog tag

by Kristal Wick

Your pet never looked so good, Dahhhhling! Replace
the doggie bones with little fish charms for kitty stylin'.
The ultimate in posh pet couture!

MATERIALS

- 1 sterling silver oblong dog tag
- Black epoxy clay
- 24 to 30 pink, orange, and crystal AB chatons in various shapes and sizes
- 2 silver doggy bone charms
- 1 silver heart charm
- 1 large silver lobster clasp
- 1 large silver jump ring

TOOLS

- Hand cream or disposable gloves
- Nonstick surface
- Anvil or steel bench block
- Letter stamp punch set
- Hammer
- Permanent black marker
- Pro-Polish Polishing Pads
- Tweezers or beeswax applicator (optional, for picking up chatons)
- 2 pairs of flat-nose pliers

1 Stamp your dog's name onto the tag as follows. Place the dog tag on an anvil or bench block. Place the letter punch on the tag and hold the punch straight up (see Tip). Hit the punch hard with a heavy hammer, being careful not to move the punch. The goal is to hit it only once, but you can hit again if you think the punch didn't make a deep impression.

tip Spacing the little letters can be tricky, so you might want to write the name out on a piece of paper vertically to use as a template. You'd be surprised how many typos can come up without this little helper! Start by stamping the middle letter and working up from there, then working down from the middle, and you're sure to have the name placed in the center of the tag.

2 Color inside the letters with the permanent marker. Rub off excess ink from the tag surface with the polishing pad. This gives the recessed letters definition so you can read them.

3 Roll out a small ball of black epoxy clay A and add an equal amount of epoxy clay B. Mix according to the manufacturer's instructions.

4 Roll out pea-size balls of clay and smush them randomly around the edges of the tag, being careful not to cover the name. Jam and cram chatons and charms into the clay balls, and then let the clay thoroughly cure.

5 Attach the clasp to the tag with a jump ring.

bling bangle

by Debra Saucier

Cotton candy comes to mind with this cuff. It's a beaut from every angle—pretty in pink with a dash of class!

MATERIALS

- White epoxy clay
- 1 channel-set bangle bracelet, approximately 1 inch (2.5 cm) wide
- 225 to 250 purple, pink, red, and clear crystal stones in a variety of shapes and sizes

TOOLS

- Hand cream or disposable gloves
- Nonstick surface
- Tweezers or beeswax applicator (optional, for picking up chatons)

1 Roll out 1 ounce (28 g) of white epoxy clay and add an equal amount of epoxy clay B. Mix according to the manufacturer's instructions.

2 Roll the clay mixture into a log. Place the clay log in the channel on one side of the bangle bracelet, between the clasp and the spring. Push the clay to the outer edges of the bezel. Smooth the clay using a light feathering motion with your fingertips. To make a tapered rounded edge around the bangle, press one fingertip at an angle around all the edges once you've finished smoothing.

3 Place all of the larger crystals around the bracelet, spacing them as desired. Use a beeswax applicator to place the smaller crystals, filling in the spaces.

4 Repeat steps 1 through 3 with the other side of the bangle.

5 Let the clay fully cure.

These seared-edge fabric
flowers are so fun to make,
you'll fear becoming a
pyromaniac. Attached by
a removable pin/pendant
finding to a lariat, your floral
pièce de résistance can also
be worn as a pin.

by Kristal Wick

flower power lariat

MATERIALS

- Black epoxy clay
- Large cosmic oval ring crystal, 33 x 24 mm
- 4 pink chatons, 1.9 mm
- 2 blue chatons, 2.6 mm
- 1¼-inch (3.2 cm) length of pink cup chain, 1.9 mm
- 2-inch (5.1 cm) length of crystal cup chain, 1.9 mm, cut in half
- Small amounts of sheer synthetic fabrics in a variety of colors
- Fabric glue
- Two-part epoxy glue
- Felt
- Pin/pendant finding
- Beading thread
- Seed beads in a wide variety of colors, size 8°
- Pink crystal bicones, 4 mm

TOOLS

- Hand cream or disposable gloves
- Nonstick surface
- Tweezers or beeswax applicator (optional, for picking up chatons)
- Fabric scissors
- Small candle
- Match or candle lighter
- Beading needle

1 Roll out a small ball of black epoxy clay A and add an equal amount of epoxy clay B. Mix according to the manufacturer's instructions.

2 Smush the clay into the center of the oval ring crystal. Using tweezers or a beeswax applicator if desired, jam the chatons and the cup chain into the clay in the pattern shown in the photo. Allow the clay to completely cure.

3 With fabric scissors, cut the sheer fabric into circles of various sizes, going from large to small.

4 Light the candle with a match or lighter and sear the edges of each circle by very carefully placing the edges near, not in, the flame and turning. The heat will seal the cut fabric and make the edges curl inward.

5 Stack the circles in size order with the largest on the bottom and glue them together with fabric glue. Let the glue dry.

6 Using the two-part epoxy, glue the oval ring crystal into the center of your fabric flower. Let the glue cure.

7 Cut a round piece of felt to fit the back of the flower and glue it in place with fabric glue. Let the glue dry.

8 Using two-part epoxy, glue the pin/pendant finding to the felt circle on the back of the flower.

9 Thread a beading needle with beading thread and make a tubular herringbone lariat with fringe 40 to 60 inches (1 to 1.5 m) long, depending on your length preference, using seed beads and crystal bicones. Pin the flower onto the lariat.

ombre rock
pendant

It's easy to get this ombre
shading effect with epoxy
clay. And the pretty wire
coils in the chain are like
potato chips—you can't
do just a few! You've
been warned!

by Kristal Wick

MATERIALS

- Epoxy clay in orange and white
- 1 crystal pendant, 48 mm
- 2 light topaz chatons, 3 mm
- 3 light topaz chatons, about 2.8 mm
- 4 light topaz chatons, about 2.5 mm
- 3 light topaz chatons, about 1.8 mm
- 10 light topaz chatons, about 1.5 mm
- 30-inch (76.2 cm) length of ice blue 20-gauge wire
- 12 peach crystal briolettes, 6 mm
- 6 multicolored and multifaceted oval crystals, 22 x 16 mm
- 42-inch (1.1 m) length of seafoam green 20-gauge wire
- 24 green-blue AB bicones, 4 mm
- 12 peach glass pearls, 6 mm
- 6 peach glass pearls, 8 mm
- 19 antique copper jump rings, 10 mm
- 1 antique copper pinch bail
- 1 copper S-hook link

TOOLS

- Hand cream or disposable gloves
- Nonstick surface
- Tweezers or beeswax applicator (optional, for picking up chatons)
- Flush wire cutters
- Round-nose pliers
- 2 pairs of flat-nose pliers

1 Make three different shades of coral clay to achieve the ombre effect (see page 12) as follows: Roll out a small to medium ball of orange epoxy clay A and divide it into three balls. Add a small ball of white epoxy clay A to one of the orange balls and mix. Add a larger ball of white to a second ball of orange epoxy clay A and mix; repeat with a larger ball of white for the third orange ball. When you're satisfied with the shades of coral, add an equal amount of epoxy clay B to each epoxy clay A ball and mix them according to the manufacturer's instructions.

2 Choose an area of the pendant to cover with clay. Roll out a long snake of the darkest shade and gently smush it onto the bottom portion of the selected area. Repeat with the other two shades with the lightest at the top and gently smooth out the edges with your fingers until you're pleased with the effect.

3 Jam chatons into the lightest clay band as follows: one 3 mm, one 2.8 mm, two 2.5 mm, one 1.8 mm, and three 1.5 mm. Jam chatons into the medium clay band as follows: one 3 mm, one 2.8 mm, one 2.5 mm, one 1.8 mm, and three 1.5 mm. Jam chatons into the darkest clay band as follows: one 2.8 mm, one 2.5 mm, one 1.8 mm, and four 1.5 mm. Allow the clay to completely cure.

4 Cut six pieces of ice blue wire about 5 inches (12.7 cm) each. To create the first spiral, fold one piece of wire in half and bend a tiny loop on one end of the wire using the tips of the round-nose pliers. Put the loop on its side inside flat-nose pliers with the wire facing out, and slowly roll the wire around the loop to create a spiral. Stop ½ inch (1.3 cm) from the bend and unfold the remaining wire. Slip one briolette, one oval crystal, and one briolette onto the wire, and then make a spiral in the opposite direction on the other end. Repeat to make five more matching pieces.

5 Cut six pieces of seafoam green wire about 7 inches (17.8 cm) each. Make six spiral components as in step 4, adding the following beads to the wires: one bicone, one 6-mm pearl, one bicone, one 8-mm pearl, one bicone, one 6-mm pearl, and one bicone.

6 Beginning with a pearl component and ending with a crystal component, use jump rings to connect three pearl components to three crystal components in an alternating pattern. Attach a chain of four jump rings to one end.

7 Squeeze the pinch bail over the hole in the pendant and slip the four jump rings through the bail. Attach components for the second half of the necklace to mirror the first half.

8 Attach four jump rings to one end link and attach the S-hook link to the other end link with a jump ring.

the joy of nature
pendant

Wood balances out the bling in this stunning pendant with a timeless, ornate quality. The enamel flower adds a charming touch to the composition.

by Katerina Ilieva

MATERIALS

- Silver flower pendant, 2.5 mm
- Ceramic paint in red and green (or any paint that will work on metal)
- Gold epoxy clay
- Metallic gold pigment powder
- Assortment of brown chatons
- Jewelry adhesive
- Wooden scallop doily embellishment, 3⅛ inches (7.9 cm) in diameter
- 10 clear flat-back crystal rhinestones, 8 x 4 mm
- 5 golden brown flat-back crystal rhinestones, 4 mm
- 5 light green flat-back crystal rhinestones, 4 mm
- 41-inch (1 m) length of black cord or chain

TOOLS

- Nonstick surface
- Toothpicks
- Petroleum jelly
- Plastic tube (to use as a roller)
- Plastic texture plate with a waves design
- Dust mask
- Tweezers or beeswax applicator (optional, for picking up chatons)
- Tweezers
- Soft cloth

1 Use a toothpick to paint the flower pendant in red and green with the ceramic paints, following the manufacturer's instructions if baking is required for the ceramic paint.

2 Apply a thin coat of petroleum jelly to your work surface, the plastic tube, the plastic texture plate, and your hands.

3 Roll out a ball of epoxy clay A and add an equal amount of epoxy clay B. Mix according to the manufacturer's instructions (the mixed clay, when rolled into a ball, should be about the size of a large gumball).

4 Wearing a dust mask, sprinkle the gold pigment powder onto the surface. Roll the clay ball to pick up all the powder.

5 With your palm, gently press the clay ball onto the work surface to create a circular shape. Use the plastic tube as a roller to flatten the clay into a pancake, about ¼ inch (6 mm) thick. To add more sparkle, sprinkle some more pigment powder onto the clay and smooth the entire surface with your fingers coated with petroleum jelly.

6 Use your fingers to push the edges of the clay inward to create a perfect circle.

7 Place the plastic texture plate on the surface of the clay, use the tube to roll it onto the clay, and then remove the plate, leaving a textured surface behind.

8 Press the flower pendant down into the clay's surface. With the tweezers or the beeswax applicator, pick up a chaton and press it into the clay until the girdle is just below the clay surface. Embed the assortment of brown chatons into the clay around the pendant. Use tweezers to adjust the chatons if necessary.

9 Leave the clay to cure for three hours and then spread an even layer of jewelry adhesive over the entire back of the clay. Glue the clay onto the center of the wooden doily embellishment.

10 With the tweezers, turn the flat-back rhinestone crystals upside down. Add a drop of jewelry adhesive to the back of each with a toothpick. Glue the rhinestones to the wooden frame one by one. Set the piece aside and let the glue dry and the clay cure completely for 24 hours.

11 Use a damp cloth to wipe all the crystals.

12 Finish the pendant by adding a black cord necklace or chain of your choice.

by Katerina Ilieva

filigree pendant
necklace

This vintage rose medallion exudes the glamour and grace of bygone silver screen beauties. Think Grace Kelly, Rita Hayworth, and Eva Gabor!

MATERIALS

- 56 antique brass 18-gauge open jump rings, 5 x 5 mm
- 16 antique brass filigree links, 15 x 15 mm
- 1 antique brass-plated lobster clasp, 9.5 x 5.5 mm
- 1 antique brass filigree pendant, 60 x 60 mm
- Green-gold metallic rub-on paste
- 16 clear flat-back crystal rhinestones, about 2.4 mm
- Jewelry adhesive
- Red epoxy clay
- 6 clear crystal chatons, about 3.1 mm
- 32 clear crystal chatons, about 1.8 mm
- 28 clear crystal chatons, about 2.6 mm

TOOLS

- Petroleum jelly (optional, see Tip)
- Nonstick surface
- Chain-nose pliers
- Flat-nose pliers
- Tweezers or beeswax applicator (optional, for picking up chatons)
- Toothpicks
- Plastic tube (as roller)
- Needle tool with sharp point
- Ball stylus
- Soft cloth

1 Using chain-nose and flat-nose pliers to open the jump rings, connect the filigree links with jump rings to make two chains with eight links each. Attach jump rings to all four of the ending filigree corners.

2 Connect more jump rings to one end of each chain until you have the desired length of chain. Attach one half of the clasp to each end of the jump-ring chain. Don't attach the pendant yet.

3 If desired, highlight the surface of the chain and the filigree pendant on both sides by applying metallic paste with your fingers. When you're finished, wash your hands.

4 Use tweezers to turn all of the flat-back crystal rhinestones upside down. With a toothpick, add a drop of jewelry adhesive to the back of the rhinestones. Glue one rhinestone to the center of each filigree link. Prop the chain up on its side and leave for 24 hours, allowing the glue and metallic paste to dry completely.

5 Roll out a large gumball-size amount of epoxy clay A and add an equal amount of epoxy clay B. Mix according to manufacturer's instructions. Roll the clay into a ball with your hands, then gently press on the ball to create a circular shape. Use the plastic tube as a roller to flatten the clay into a pancake about 2 ¾ inches (7 cm) in diameter and ³⁄₁₆ inch (4.5 mm) thick. Smooth the entire surface of the clay.

tip

Katerina uses petroleum jelly to coat her nonstick work surface, roller, and hands before working with the epoxy clay. She also uses a bit on her fingers when smoothing the surface of her clay creations.

filigree pendant necklace

6 Press the filigree pendant front-side-down into the clay patty until about 2 mm of the clay comes up through the holes of the pendant and about 1 mm of thickness remains on the back. Remove any excess clay from the edges of the pendant using a toothpick or the needle tool.

7 Holding the pendant in one hand with the back facing you, use your fingers to smooth the edges and the back. Use the ball stylus to press random dots into the back, creating a textured surface (see photo, page 119). Place the pendant on the work surface with the front facing up.

8 With the beeswax applicator, pick up the chatons and press them into the clay until the girdle is just below the clay's surface, first embedding the largest chatons in the center, then embedding the smallest chatons in the middle area, and finally embedding

the midsize chatons along the edge of the pendant. Use tweezers to adjust the chatons as needed.

9 Use the needle tool to make small holes on each side of the pendant, as shown in the photo—these holes will be used to connect the pendant to the chain with jump rings.

10 Use the needle tool to stipple the clay, either following the design in this piece shown or allowing yourself to be inspired by the design of your filigree.

11 Prop the pendant on its side and leave for 24 hours to allow the clay to cure completely.

12 When the pendant has cured, use chain-nose and flat-nose pliers to connect the chain and the pendant with the jump rings.

13 Use a damp cloth to wipe all the crystals clean.

madonna
necklace

It's hard to believe this pendant isn't stolen from the Louvre! Epoxy clay makes image transfer easy with just a color photocopy.

by Debbi Simon

madonna necklace

MATERIALS

- 26-gauge brass sheet, ⅜ x 12 inches (1 x 30.5 cm)
- Template
- 2 rivets, ⅛ inch (3 mm)
- 12-inch (30.5 cm) length of 24-gauge copper wire
- Images (see Note)
- 2 color photocopies (see Note)
- White epoxy clay
- 3 brass nail heads, ⅛ inch (3 mm)
- 9 clear rectangular crystals, 6 x 2 mm
- 8 bronze crystal foil-backed chatons, 2.5 mm
- 24-inch (61 cm) length of chain
- 2 copper spacers with ⅛-inch (3 mm) holes
- 2 barbell links, 1 inch (2.5 cm)

TOOLS

- Hand cream or disposable gloves
- Nonstick surface
- Nylon-jaw pliers
- Round-nose pliers
- Flat-nose pliers
- Flush wire cutters
- File or sandpaper
- Drill with ⅛-inch (3 mm) twist drill bit
- Bench block
- Riveting hammer
- Scissors
- Metal spoon
- Tweezers or beeswax applicator (optional, for picking up chatons)
- Small bowl of water at room temperature (optional)
- Butane torch (optional)

Note: Debbi used copyright-free images of Renaissance art. The transferred image will be the reverse of the original image, so if orientation is important, scan and flip the image on your computer before making the working copy. Laser or toner-based printer copies usually work best for image transfer. If you only have access to an inkjet printer, test an image from it on a scrap piece of epoxy clay first.

Make the Bezel

1 Using the nylon-jaw pliers, round-nose pliers, and flat-nose pliers, bend the brass sheet to match the template, starting at the points noted. Be sure to gently curve the piece on the two sides and overlap at the bottom to match the template. Use flush wire cutters to trim off any excess, and then use a file or sandpaper to smooth the edges so there are no sharp points.

2 Drill two holes for the join as shown in figure 1. Overlap and line up the ends. Using the drilled holes as a guide, mark the holes for the other end of the brass and drill them. Drill three holes on top for the nail heads.

3 Line up the rivet holes and insert the rivets so the nail head is on the outside. With the nail head down on the bench block, trim the rivet to 2 mm above where it exits the inside. Use the riveting hammer to form a nail head on the inside wire you just trimmed by tapping lightly so it spreads out slightly over the hole and gradually increasing the intensity of the taps until both pieces are secure. With the flat side of the hammer, give one final pound to make sure the joint is secure.

4 Wrap the copper wire tightly eight to 10 times around one top bezel edge (see figure 1).

Fill the Bezel

1 Make color photocopies of the copyright-free images. Trim the color photocopies to match the size of your bezel with a little overlap. Cut out the area on one image where the crystals will be placed.

2 Roll out a ball of white epoxy clay A and add an equal amount of epoxy clay B. Mix according to the manufacturer's instructions. Make sure you've mixed enough clay to fill the bezel, but don't place it in the bezel yet.

3 Lay one color copy face up on the nonstick surface. The color copy will act as the back of the bezel for now. Center the metal bezel form on top of the color copy. Fill the bezel with epoxy clay by rolling the clay into a ball and pushing it down into the form, and then stretching the clay out to completely fill the bezel and completely cover the color copy. Be sure to push the clay into the corners of the bezel. The bezel should be almost full.

The working time for the clay is up to three hours, but creating transfers relies on the adhesive quality of the clay. Stretching the clay as opposed to compressing it to fill the bezel will leave the clay tackier.

4 When you have a nice even fill in your bezel, use your fingers to smooth out the clay until you have an even surface, but don't smooth too much—doing so can leave the clay less tacky. Center the second color copy face down on top of the bezel form filled with clay. Burnish the paper with the back of a spoon so it is completely touching the clay. The better the seal, the better the transfer.

5 Insert the three brass nail heads into the clay through the drilled holes on top of the bezel.

6 Use the tweezers or the beeswax applicator to place the rectangular and small round crystals in the cutout area of the appropriate image. Put the piece aside and let it completely cure.

7 When the piece is cured, use your fingers to dab water liberally on the back of the paper on one side of the clay-filled bezel and allow it to sit for five minutes. Dab more water onto the paper and start rubbing your fingers over the paper to remove it from the clay. The color image will remain on the clay after all the paper is removed.

8 Remove the paper from the other side of the bezel and wipe any excess water off both sides of the bezel.

Add the Chain

1 If desired, heat the chain with the hot part of the flame from a butane torch to alter and patina it. Be sure to work in a well-ventilated area following safety precautions.

2 Singe the chain with water.

3 Mark and drill two holes in the upper corners for the chain to be added.

4 Insert a spacer, the end link of the chain, and a barbell link into each drilled hole, and screw the ends onto the barbell link, securing the chain to the pendant.

Barbell links can be found in body-piercing stores. They consist of a small wire with ball head screws on each end. They make a fun addition to the findings you work with.

template

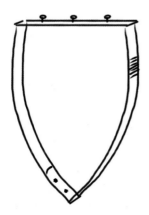

figure 1

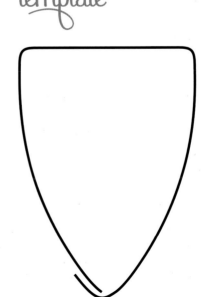

by Debbi Simon

vintage filigree necklace

Epoxy goes sophisticated. Filigree components encasing subtle shades of epoxy clay and complementary chains give this piece a quiet elegance.

MATERIALS

- Epoxy clay in white, red, green, yellow, and blue
- 1 brass teardrop full droplet filigree wrap bead, 27 x 9 mm
- 1 Etruscan brass filigree drop, 27 x 9 mm
- 1 ball head pin, 2 inches (5.1 cm)
- 2 filigree squares (one dapped), 20 mm
- 1 round filigree bead wrap, 15 mm
- 1 flat filigree circle, 20 mm
- 4 round filigree beads, 10 mm
- 1 oval filigree bead, 15 mm
- 3 brass eye pins
- 1 extra brass jump ring, 5 mm (optional, see Assemble the Necklace, step 1)
- 30-inch (76.2 cm) length of brass or copper cable chain, 4 mm
- 10 brass jump rings, 5 mm
- 24-inch (61 cm) length of brass or copper rollo chain, 2.5 mm
- 1 brass toggle clasp

TOOLS

- Hand cream or disposable gloves
- Nonstick surface
- Chain-nose pliers
- Alcohol or baby wipes
- Round-nose pliers
- Bail-making pliers (optional)
- Flush wire cutters

Make the Clay Colors

1 Mix together amounts of epoxy clay A in white, red, green, yellow, and blue as follows to create salmon, teal, and lavender clay. Note: 1 part = pea-size ball.

Teal: 3 parts blue, 1 part green, and 1 part white.

Salmon: 3 parts red, 1 part yellow, 1 part white, and a touch of blue.

Lavender: 2 parts blue, 1 part red, and 1 part white.

Set the balls of colored epoxy clay A aside.

Make the Teardrop Filigree Bead

1 Use chain-nose pliers to open the teardrop filigree wrap bead so that it looks like an X, then partially close the four sides back to a point where you can still fill the cavity with clay.

2 Mix some teal epoxy clay A with an equal amount of epoxy clay B according to the manufacturer's instructions. The mixed clay should be enough to fill the cavity of the teardrop.

3 Push the clay into the cavity without pushing it through the filigree lacework. Slowly close the teardrop shape around the clay. If you have too much clay, open the filigree just enough to remove the excess clay. Once the teardrop is closed and there's no excess clay, secure the top of the filigree with a clip of some sort to hold the shape. Use alcohol or a baby wipe to clean the filigree of any excess clay or residue. Set the piece aside to fully cure.

Make the Estruscan Bail

1 Take the Etruscan brass filigree drop and use the round-nose pliers and bail-making pliers to gently curl the top edge toward the back until it touches the back of the filigree, making a bail for the chain.

2 Mix some lavender epoxy clay A with an equal amount of epoxy clay B according to the manufacturer's instructions. The mixed clay should be enough to fill the shape of the Etruscan filigree.

3 Press a thin layer of the mixed lavender clay onto the back of the filigree without pushing it through the filigree. Use the head pin to make a hole near the bottom of the piece (this will be used to hang the teardrop bead), removing the head pin before the clay cures fully. Use alcohol or a baby wipe to clean the filigree and the head pin of any excess clay or residue. Set the head pin aside for now and the filigree bail aside to fully cure.

Make the Decorative Filigree Beads

1 Gather the two filigrees squares, one that is flat and one that is dapped. If you can't find a dapped square, you can dap it yourself with a dapping block.

2 Mix some teal epoxy clay A with an equal amount of epoxy clay B. The mixed clay should be enough to fill the cavity created when you hold the two squares together.

3 Press a thin layer of clay onto each square, making sure you cover the pieces all the way to the corners. Sandwich the two squares together, adding more clay if necessary so they come together securely. Be sure not to press the clay through the filigree. Use alcohol or a baby wipe to clean the filigree of any excess clay or residue. Set the piece aside to fully cure.

4 Use chain-nose pliers to open the round filigree bead wrap so it looks like an X. Mix some salmon epoxy clay A with an equal amount of epoxy clay B. The mixed clay should be enough to fill the cavity of the bead.

5 Press a thin layer of clay onto the back of the bead, again making sure that the clay doesn't get pushed through the filigree.

6 Place the filled bead on top of the filigree circle, sandwiching the clay between the two pieces. Wrap the edges of the bead slightly around the circle if necessary to secure the pieces together. Use alcohol or a baby wipe to clean the filigree of any excess clay or residue. Set the piece aside to fully cure.

7 Mix some salmon epoxy clay A with an equal amount of epoxy clay B according to the manufacturer's instructions. The mixed clay should be enough to fill the cavity of one 10-mm round filigree bead.

8 Push the clay through the filigree into the cavity without opening the bead. Continue until the bead is filled, keeping the outside of the filigree as clean as possible. Use alcohol or a baby wipe to clean the filigree of any excess clay or residue. Push a head pin through the bead hole to make sure the hole is still open, remove the head pin, and set the piece aside to fully cure.

9 Repeat steps 7 and 8 to fill two 10-mm round beads with teal, one 10-mm round bead with lavender, and the 15-mm oval bead with lavender. Don't set these aside to cure—proceed to the next step before they cure.

Prepare the Beads for Hanging

1 Pass an eye pin through the oval bead; with wire cutters, cut the eye pin about ½ inch (1.3 cm) from the bead and use round-nose pliers to form a simple loop (see page 14).

2 Pass an eye pin through the salmon filigree bead and one teal filigree bead. Cut the eye pin about ½ inch (1.3 cm) from the beads and use round-nose pliers to form a simple loop.

3 Pass an eye pin through the lavender filigree bead and the remaining teal filigree bead. Cut the eye pin about ½ inch (1.3 cm) from the beads and use round-nose pliers to form a simple loop.

Assemble the Necklace

1 To use the ball head pin to attach the teardrop to the Etruscan filigree bail, first pass the head pin through the bottom hole at the front of the bail. Then pass it through the connector at the top of the teardrop. Use round-nose pliers to bend the head pin and press it as close to the back of the bail as possible, and then form a small loop. Trim off any extra wire and press the loop beneath the curved top of the bail for security. (For a slightly different look and easier assembly, you could also just attach the teardrop to the bail with a jump ring!)

2 Cut approximately 15 inches (38 cm) of the cable chain and pass it through the bail.

3 With the bail centered, use a jump ring to attach one link of the chain that's about 2½ inches (6.4 cm) to the left of the bail to the lower corner of the square piece, then use a jump ring to attach a link an equal distance from the bail on the right side to the circle piece. Make sure the chain lies nicely and that you like the space between the three pieces as they hang.

4 Attach one link of the chain to the next corner of the square piece with a jump ring, creating a loop in the chain as shown in the photos. Repeat on the other side, attaching the chain to the circle piece with another jump ring to form another loop.

5 Open the eye pin loops to attach the left end of the cable chain to the salmon and teal bead set and the right end of the chain to the lavender and teal bead set.

6 Cut two 2-inch (5.1 cm) pieces of the rollo chain. Open the eye pin loops on the oval bead and attach one end of each length of chain to a loop. Attach the end the chain on the left of the oval bead to the top corner of the square piece with a jump ring. Attach the end of the other length of chain to the circle piece with a jump ring. Check to make sure you like the arrangement and lengths.

7 Cut the leftover cable chain into two equal lengths; repeat for the rollo chain.

8 Use jump rings to attach one length of the rollo chain to the remaining corner of the square and the other length of rollo chain to the remaining loop of the circle piece. Attach the lengths of cable chain to the open ends of the two-bead sets.

9 Use one jump ring to attach one end of the cable chain and one end of the rollo chain to one half of the toggle clasp. Repeat to attach the other chains to the other half of the clasp.

This cleverly constructed shadow box pendant uses the image-transfer technique on mica to create beautiful windows you can peek through to view the tiny charms within.

by Debbi Simon

shadow box necklace

MATERIALS

- White epoxy clay
- Variety of rubber stamp ink, oil and acrylic paints, dyes, and/or rub-on pastes
- 16 nail heads in a variety of sizes
- Color photocopy (see Note)
- Packing tape
- 4 mica sheets (each sheet should be larger than the inside circle of the metal stamping but smaller than its outside diameter)
- 2 round metal stampings, open in the center
- Two-part epoxy glue
- Trinkets for inside the box, including fun crystal shapes
- 1 eye pin, trimmed to 1 inch (2.5 cm)
- 24-inch (61 cm) length of decorative chain
- Jump ring

Note: Debbi used a copyright-free image of Renaissance art. The transferred image will be the reverse of the original image, so if orientation is important, scan and flip the image on your computer before making the working copy. Laser or toner-based printer copies usually work best for image transfer. If you only have access to an inkjet printer, test an image from it on a scrap piece of epoxy clay first.

TOOLS

- Olive oil
- Nonstick surface
- Rolling pin
- Rubber stamps or texture sheets
- 2 round cookie cutters, 2¼ inches and 1 inch (5.7 and 2.5 cm)
- Metal spoon
- Craft knife
- File or sandpaper
- Damp rag or paper towel
- Scissors
- Bowl of room temperature water
- Black fine-tip permanent marker
- Drill with ⅛-inch (3 mm) bit
- Awl or other sharp tool for piercing mica
- 2 pairs of flat-nose pliers

Make the Clay Box

1 Lightly oil the nonstick sheet, rolling pin, rubber stamps or texture sheets, cookie cutters and your hands.

2 Roll out a small ball of white epoxy clay A and add an equal amount of epoxy clay B (the two balls together should equal about the size of a golf ball). Mix according to the manufacturer's instructions. Flatten the ball out on the nonstick surface to ½ inch (1.3 cm) thick with the rolling pin.

3 Peel the clay off the nonstick surface, being careful not to stretch it, and place it on a rubber stamp or texture sheet that's facing texture side up. (For added detail and dimension, stamp the rubber stamp with rubber stamp ink or brush it with paint or rub-on paste.) Gently push the clay down into the stamp—far enough to create the texture but not so far or hard that you'll have trouble separating the clay from the rubber stamp.

4 Place another prepared rubber stamp or texture sheet onto the back of the clay and lightly burnish it with the back of a metal spoon, making a "texture sandwich." Again, don't push down too hard or you'll have trouble peeling the clay from the stamps.

5 Set the clay aside for half an hour—the clay will start to cure—then carefully remove the top stamp only. Don't get impatient! If you try to remove the stamp earlier, the clay will be too tacky and will stretch and distort.

6 Use the large round cookie cutter to cut out a large circle shape, leaving the bottom rubber stamp in place. Remove the excess clay from around the edges. Use the small round cookie cutter to cut a circle from the center of the circle of clay. Clean and trim off excess clay with a craft knife so you have a neat ring of clay.

shadow box necklace

packing tape. Burnish the copy to the tape with the back of a metal spoon.

3 With your fingers, dab water liberally onto the paper side of the tape, and allow it to sit for five minutes.

4 Dab more water onto the paper and start rubbing your fingers over the back of the copy to remove the paper. The color image will be left behind on the packing tape. Continue adding water and rubbing until all the paper is removed. Dry off the packing tape.

5 Sandwich the transfer between two of the mica sheets.

Finish the Box

1 Using one metal stamping as a guide, trim off any excess packing tape or mica so the transfer-and-mica sandwich fits behind the metal stamping.

7 Insert nail heads into the outside edge of the shape, reserving at least eight for finishing. Allow the piece to completely cure.

8 Remove the bottom rubber stamp and clean up the edges of the shape with a file or sandpaper.

> **tip** Sometimes Debbi takes off a little more clay with the sandpaper to give a piece an aged and weathered look.

9 Use a variety of paints and dyes to color and accent the textured details. First coat the piece with a color and then use a rag or paper towel to remove it immediately from the raised areas, leaving it in the recesses. Gently rub other highlighting colors onto the raised areas of the piece. Have fun with this part—this is where you can really make it your own. Set the piece aside to dry.

Make the Paper Transfer

1 Trim the color photocopy so it's slightly larger than the small inner circle of the cured clay ring.

2 Cut a piece of packing tape slightly larger than the cutout photocopy. Place the photocopy with the color side down onto the sticky side of the

2 Center the metal stamping over the opening of the clay ring and use the marker to mark the locations for the nails that will attach the metal stamping.

3 Remove the metal stamping and use the drill with the ⅛-inch (3 mm) bit to drill the holes in the metal stamping for the nails. Use the metal stamping as a template to mark the clay ring for the hole locations. Drill holes into the clay ring.

4 Center the mica sandwich onto the back of the metal stamping. Line up the drill holes on the metal stamping and the clay shape (piercing the mica with a sharp tool, if necessary) and attach the nails with the two-part epoxy glue, following the manufacturer's instructions for the glue.

5 Turn the box over and add small trinkets—include a few crystals to liven up the group. Make sure the elements can move around inside.

6 Repeat these steps to attach the two plain sheets of mica and the second metal stamping to the back of the box.

7 Drill a hole in the top of the box and glue in the eye pin with two-part epoxy glue. Once the glue sets, open the eye pin with two pairs of flat-nose pliers and attach the chain with a jump ring.

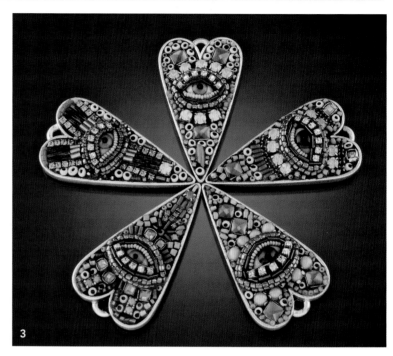

1 LINDA HARTUNG
WIRELACE FLOATING FLOWERS

2 BRENDA SCHWEDER
SPILLING OUT

3 BETSY YOUNGQUIST
EYE HEART PENDANTS

4 BETSY YOUNGQUIST
GEORGE

5 BETSY YOUNGQUIST
THREE LITTLE BIRDS

6 LAURA ANN TIMMONS
GOLDEN CRYSTAL SURPRISE

7 JAMIE NORTH
OVER A BARREL

8 BETSY YOUNGQUIST
BEADED TOP PENDANTS

9 BETSY YOUNGQUIST
DANCING BOY

10 DIANE FITZGERALD
NINE HEARTS PENDANTS

about the author

Residing in Colorado, international award-winning designer and Swarovski ambassador Kristal Wick has been represented in galleries spanning the globe, including Canyon Road in Santa Fe, New Mexico; Alaska; the Cayman Islands; Italy; Germany; and the Virgin Islands.

Previously the editor of BeadingDaily.com, Kristal is the author of the books *Sassy Silky Savvy*, *Fabulous Fabric Beads* (a bestseller in five categories on Amazon.com), and the forthcoming *Metal Clay 101 for Beaders*. Kristal also has two DVDs: *Mixed Media: Beaded Bracelets with Fiber Beads, Crystals, Resin*, and *Wire and Mixed Media:*

Jewelry Making with Handmade Beads, Crystals, Resin, and More!

A jewelry design expert and blogger, Kristal teaches worldwide at quilt and bead shows and on cruise ships. She has created jewelry for the Jimmy Buffet Band, Ali MacGraw, and Marianne Williamson. She is a frequent guest on HGTV and PBS, and her designs have been featured in over 45 publications, including *Belle Armoire*, *Vogue Patterns*, *Lapidary Journal*, *Stringing*, *Beadwork*, *Bead Style*, *Crafts Business*, *Simply Beads*, *SewNews*, *Sewing Savvy*, *Piecework*, *Step by Step Beads*, *Crafts Report*, *Crafts-n-Things*, and *Bead Design Studio*.

Photo by Chris Orlikowski

Kristal is available for guild and shop book signings, workshops, lectures, trunk shows, and freelance design. Sign up for her free online newsletter at KristalWick.com.

acknowledgments

It takes a village to create a book. Thanks to "my village" from the bottom of my blingy little toes!

Swarovski Elements, Fire Mountain Gems, Aves, Crystal Clay, Decore, Clear Snap, Plaid, Beadalon, KatyDids, Ala Carte Clasp and WireLace, Tierra Cast, Vintaj, Nunn Designs, Green Girl, HHH Enterprises, Susan Lenart Kazmer, Garlan Chain, Ogilvie, Inc., Bead Trust, Metal Me This, Tinsel Trading Company, CJS Sales Ltd., Ranger, and Beads Gone Wild for their priceless product donation.

Also thanks to: Chris Orlikowski for her genius and artistic generosity; the Lark Jewelry & Beading group for making this book so fab; my four-legged fur babies, Sparkle and Bling, who constantly inspire and lick me (in that order); and a big old hug to all the folks who've taken my classes, visited my blog and website, or bought this book. You all help this boho-ista live her dream each and every day!

credits

EDITOR
Kathy Sheldon

ART DIRECTOR
Carol Morse Barnao

PROJECT PHOTOGRAPHY
Lynne Harty

ILLUSTRATOR
Orrin Lundgren

COVER DESIGNER
Carol Morse Barnao

EDITORIAL ASSISTANCE
Hannah Doyle

index